POPULATION DYNAMICS AND FAMILY PLANNING:

A NEW RESPONSIBILITY FOR SOCIAL WORK EDUCATION

Edited by Katherine A. Kendall

Proceedings of an International Conference on Social Work Education, Population, and Family Planning

March 8-13, 1970
East-West Center, Hawaii

Sponsored by the Council on Social Work Education in cooperation with the East-West Center and funded by the Agency for International Development

COUNCIL ON SOCIAL WORK EDUCATION
345 East 46th Street, New York N. Y. 10017

Library of Congress No. 78-151623

X343

Foreword

The International Conference on Social Work Education, Population, and Family Planning, Sponsored by the Council on Social Work Education in cooperation with the East-West Center, Hawaii, was held from March 8-13, 1970, in Honolulu. The Conference was made possible by a grant from the Agency for International Development which recognized the need for a stronger emphasis on social factors and social work manpower in this field.

While the Conference had as its main purpose the awakening of U.S. schools of social work to an urgent new responsibility, it had the benefit of international participation. The 104 delegates came from 28 countries, with every geographical region represented. In keeping with the locale and purpose of the Conference, however, the bulk of the participants came from North America and Asia.

The Conference was interprofessional as well as international in composition. The planning and organization of the meeting were guided by a distinguished interdisciplinary Advisory Committee of seventeen members, including representatives of the United Nations and UNICEF; governmental and non-governmental agencies; national and international organizations concerned with population policy, planned parenthood, and social welfare; leaders in medical, public health, nursing, and social work education and practice; and outstanding pioneers of the family planning movement. The Council on Social Work Education takes this opportunity to express its gratitude for the help and support accorded by the Advisory Committee to this important activity. A number of the organizations represented on the Committee went beyond the giving of advice to providing reference materials and underwriting the expenses of some of the participants. The excellent cooperation given throughout by the East-West Center and many colleagues who assisted with the planning, organization, and conduct of the meeting is also deeply appreciated.

To ensure effective international as well as national participation, responsibility for the Conference was lodged in the Division of International Education of the Council on Social Work Education. Dr. Katherine A. Kendall, CSWE Director of International Education, who also serves as Secretary-General of the International Association of Schools of Social Work, was named as project director. She has also served as editor of the Proceedings. The Council was also fortunate in having the assistance of Mrs. Katherine B. Oettinger as a special consultant in planning and coordinating the program. Mrs. Oettinger came to this assignment from the Department of Health, Education, and Welfare, where she served first as Chief of the Children's Bureau and later as Deputy Assistant for Family Planning and Population.

The Council on Social Work Education is proud to present this report of an excellent Conference which more than fulfilled the expectations of its organizers in opening up new opportunities for social work and social work education to contribute to the solution of a universal concern.

Arnulf M. Pins
Executive Director

February, 1971

Editor's Preface

"All men are brothers, all brothers are different, and the difference is beautiful." These words of welcome from Everett Kleinjans, Chancellor of the East-West Center in Hawaii, almost immediately took on symbolic significance for the 104 delegates to the International Conference on Social Work Education, Population, and Family Planning.

They came from all over the world and from a variety of disciplines to explore questions of great importance in the areas of population and family planning and to discover where the social work profession can most fruitfully make its contribution in the search for answers. The world-wide consequences of too rapid population growth and the lack of family planning information and resources were readily accepted as matters of universal concern. Equally important, however, was the recognition of the national, cultural, and professional differences that must be taken into account in organizing family planning services and in dealing with population questions. The delegates, working together in a spirit of international fraternity, clearly brought to the Conference a variety of perceptions of these problems, different approaches to their solution, and sensitive appreciation and acceptance of the desirability of the difference.

The central purposes of the Conference embodied three major tasks:

1. To bring to social work education the basic facts about population growth and its impact on the world environment and on individual countries, neighborhoods, and families.

2. To clarify the range of roles and functions that fall within the context of an effective social work contribution to population and family planning activities.
3. To produce broad recommendations for curriculum development at different levels of social work education and training, including continuing education.

How the tasks were pursued and with what excellent results are the subject of the two reports that make up the first section of the "Proceedings." The rapporteur's summary, creatively and incisively recorded by Herman D. Stein, does much more than describe what happened. Dr. Stein brings to bear his capacity for brilliant analysis and synthesis on the major speeches and reports from the discussion groups. Similarly, Irwin T. Sanders, in presenting a more detailed report and critique of the Conference, has produced an excellent essay which pulls together a wealth of material from the background material, the plenary session papers, a panel presentation, and comments by the participants.

These two reports serve as an introduction to all that follows. By virtue of their comprehensive coverage of the full range of opinions and events, however, they also stand alone as a record of the Conference. Thus, the two reports are being issued as a separate monograph concurrently with the "Proceedings" for wide distribution around the world.

The full Proceedings are published under the title *Family Planning and Population Dynamics: A New Responsibility for Social Work Education.* Part II brings together the papers presented by outstanding specialists in the fields of population, family planning, and social work. Part III includes the background papers that were distributed in advance to the participants; and Part IV reproduces the program and lists all who contributed to it together with the names of the delegates and their professional responsibilities at the time of the Conference.

The full impact of population pressures on the world environment comes through dramatically in the statistics cited by Milos Macura of the United Nations. Social workers, with their deep concern for the quality of life for people everywhere, saw clearly that social workers no less than economists, demographers, doctors, nurses, life scientists, environmentalists, and political leaders have a stake in finding solutions and a role to play.

Aida Gindy, also of the United Nations, spells out in her paper the many roles that have already been delineated by and for social workers in the countries of the developing world. She also projects a wide range of new and expanded responsibilities when the profession is ready and educationally equipped to undertake them. She particularly emphasizes the importance of interdisciplinary training and practice—a direction which was accepted in all the discussion groups. Social work educators from the United States, noting the progress that had already been made toward a more effective social work contribution in other regions, began to sense how unknowing and "underdeveloped" they must seem in conversations with their colleagues from other countries. By the end of the Conference, the American delegates not only had learned much; they realized how much more they have to learn.

Selo Soemardjan brings home in his paper the crucial significance of religious, ethical, and cultural forces and value judgments in all aspects of work in the field of population and family planning. In discussions of the dynamics of psycho-social, political, and economic change, the contribution of the social worker as practitioner, administrator, and planner emerged clearly. Social workers are already well equipped to understand and help stimulate needed change in mores and attitudes, to direct this change toward an impact on policy, and to act as a direct force for enlightened action by legislators and political administrators. How to relate this type of competence to effective work in policies, programs, and services, particularly in the area of family planning, became an agenda item for continuing consideration by social work educators.

The Conference dealt with many aspects of the population problem. It also concentrated directly on family planning, where great emphasis was placed by the social work delegates on voluntarism and freedom of choice. The papers by Alan F. Guttmacher and Antonio Ordoñez-Plaja introduced broad perspectives on both subjects which helped the delegates to understand that population control and family planning are not interchangeable concepts. The social work delegates clearly recognized family planning as an urgently needed activity in its own right, apart from any impact it might have on the population problem. Dr. Guttmacher vividly described the early days of family planning, bringing home to all the participants the tremendous transformation that has taken place in social policy and public attitudes on birth control. Again, the call for interprofessional approaches to the organization, planning, and administration of family planning services brought an interested response from the participants.

The reference materials distributed in advance were supplemented by generous donations of documents, pamphlets, and articles by a number of the organizations represented at the Conference. Many of the delegates received the papers by Lydia Rapoport and Katherine Kendall which appear as Part III of this volume. Miss Rapoport's paper is a rich source of information on social work education and practice in family planning. The basic definitions included in it help to clarify the difference between population control and family planning. Her position that family planning resources should be available to all who desire them and that population policy must be aimed at all of society and not just at the poor was reiterated again and again by the social work delegates at the Conference itself.

The Conference concluded with endorsement of the need for continuing work on the many questions that were raised but not answered. It was said repeatedly that this meeting in Hawaii was only a beginning, a first step in the direction of more work under international and regional auspices on curriculum building, faculty development, and production of teaching materials. At a later meeting of international leaders in social work education convened by the International Association of Schools of Social Work, definite proposals were put forward for this continuing work.

It was recommended that educational development in schools of social work be carried on within the context of a central plan that would encompass preparatory curriculum development by selected individual schools of social work, regional conferences, and an international curriculum workshop. The group recommended that any future project should concentrate on the curricular needs of programs of basic social work education since a major problem to be solved lies in the inadequate preparation in most countries of professional social workers for family planning and population responsibilities. Certain curriculum areas were listed as probably universal for all schools but stress was laid on the necessity of working out specific curricular content in the light of local needs and considerations. It was suggested that the international and regional meetings as well as curriculum development within individual schools of social work make effective use of representatives of other disciplines.

The Conference at the East-West Center opened many doors. The dialogue among social work educators from all parts of the world will unquestionably continue on the tasks that lie ahead and how to prepare for them. The communication that was initiated between social workers and representatives of a wide range of disciplines will perhaps become a pattern of professional education and practice in social work. The Conference was characterized by a remarkable absence of either professional or national chauvinism. Learning flowed easily in a mutually enriching interchange across cultural, national, and professional differences. At the end of the week, the delegates appreciatively remembered and applauded the opening words of greeting: "All men are brothers, all brothers are different, and the difference is beautiful."

Katherine A. Kendall

Contents

PART I: Summary and Critique

The Context of Social Work's Contribution

SUMMARY OF THE RAPPORTEUR:
HERMAN D. STEIN

INTRODUCTION

In a sense, this overview of a very vital and stimulating Conference is more in the nature of a commentary than a summary. It is based on the discussions and materials of the Conference in an effort—which must be tried, however impossible of attainment—to capture its essence, but it is of necessity selective and partial. It incorporates my own interpretations, which in context should hopefully be distinguishable from direct summary.

This Conference was most unusual and highly significant. Although nationally organized, it had the benefit of international participation and exchange. There were no prescriptions for any countries, yet the recommendations that flowed from the discussion groups undoubtedly will have impact on deliberations within many social welfare agencies and social work education institutions in many parts of the world. The function of the Conference was essentially as a starter mechanism to vitalize the role of social work education with respect to population policy and family planning and to make clear the responsibility which social workers have in family planning specifically and more generally in population policy.

The central characteristic of this Conference was an open search for direction and a realistic concern with the problems and the facts. Relatively little ambiguity and sloganeering crept in to interfere with the serious attempts to grapple with the genuine problems with which we are confronted. The Conference was characterized, too, by high involvement

---

Herman D. Stein is University vice-president and provost, Case Western Reserve University, and president of the International Association of Schools of Social Work.

and the presence of key leaders of the family planning movement, pioneers who first emerged as fighters in an era when the subjects under discussion could not easily be explored in open forums. The flavor of their activism was added to their acknowledged leadership. The Conference also incorporated a world perspective, symbolized by the presence and active participation of key spokesmen for the United Nations, by a variety of international experience in its broad array of disciplines and professions, and in its range of social work professional and educational expertise.

Some Premises and Principles

Despite the fact that there were no formal actions, a very high degree of consensus appeared in the discussion groups and in the plenary sessions. Without presuming the agreement of all, I shall note the premises on which such consensus appeared to emerge, in many cases quite rapidly:

—recognition of the grave threat to the well-being of mankind of worldwide population growth trends

—recognition of the specific deterrent of a high growth rate to the economic and social development of many of the poorer countries

—refusal to generalize about what is best or right for any particular country

—acceptance of the necessity for national population policies, with strong preference for voluntarism and choice, rather than for coercive means which remove choice

—recognition of family planning as a necessary but not sufficient approach to the reduction of the rate of population growth

—repudiation of any approach to family planning or population policy which focuses on particular groups in the population rather than on the population as a whole.

With respect to the role of social work and social work education specifically, the working premises, in addressing family planning and population, appeared to incorporate views that:

—optimize the preventive and development functions of social work

—recognize the necessity for working with and learning from other disciplines and professions without being too concerned with which is more important or central

—note the importance of advocacy

—recognize the unique value of paraprofessional case aides, volunteers, and all others not professionally educated who can be encompassed within the social welfare system

—encourage needed research in concert with other disciplines in order to acquire relevant knowledge and skill for social work's contribution

—express some concern with over-control of family planning by the medical profession in some countries, which can restrict participation in and contribution of social work to the total effort

—recognize the limited curricular space within which social work education can address knowledge, skills, issues, and values related to family planning and population, and therefore the necessity of utilizing existing curricular structure wherever possible.

We were reminded in many ways of the distinctions between conception control, fertility control, and population policy. The relation between family planning and population policy is not one on which all authorities agree. Family planning has been interpreted as a primary measure for the reduction of population growth, yet there is also an emphasis, particularly within social work, to view family planning principally as a contribution to family health, stressing the importance of having children who are wanted rather than simply reducing the number of children born. While it is generally assumed that overall reduction of the number of births would follow from the practice of family planning, this need not be true of individual families, nor, from the point of view of family health and parental choice, necessarily be its primary objective.

Our discussions noted the principle of economy of effort and economy of resources in social work's relation to family planning. Thus, although innovative programs are called for, the easiest and most immediate access of social work to family planning should be undertaken in existing services before attempting anything brand new, in utilizing shared values before introducing conflict, and in employing existing social work curricula until improved curricula can be developed. There was, in other words, a sense of capitalizing more effectively on what is now available rather than attempting to see this entire subject as having to be approached *de novo,* as having a separate identity and requiring a separate institutional auspice. We stressed that the pervasive character of the problems with which we are coping requires action and resolution with a whole network, not only of social welfare agencies, but of all institutions that deal with the well-being of populations. Wherever social workers find themselves there are ways of utilizing these conceptions, whether in community development, community organization, or in research, in all types of family activities, family counseling and welfare activities, and certainly in health settings. In other words, the focus should be on using to the hilt what we now have, in addition to attempting to break new ground.

The conference also reached a consensus on the necessary differences in approaches to the problems, not only among countries but even within countries, such as the United States. There developed a strong premise and conviction among the social work participants that social work should not be involved in means for the promotion of family planning that are selectively utilized toward particular sub-groups in the population. A policy for a population was clearly seen as a policy for the *whole* population. Finally, one should note the critical importance of an international perspective, especially in this area and certainly for social work education in the United States. It has been amply demonstrated how crucial it is to learn from others, to share experience, to discover comparative ways of looking at the problems under consideration.

CONCEPTS AND THEMES

Several concepts repeatedly emerged that bear on these principles as they apply to social work education in relation to family planning and population policy. I hold no brief for them as the most essential concepts, but rather note that they constituted themes emerging so persistently in one form or another as to require that they be identified. These concepts include the following: social change, values, power, health, knowledge and competence, and approaches for social work education. I shall comment selectively on each.

Social Change

With respect to social change, one may suggest that if there is any one concept that has been accepted by social scientists, it is that resistance to change is inevitable. If anything is important in the way of planned change it will evoke resistance. If there is no opposition, the chances are that one is not dealing with anything that is terribly significant. So the fact that in this subject area, which in many ways is revolutionary, there are marked resistances to change, not only should not surprise us but should be assumed.

These resistances were characterized in the discussions as lying especially in four categories: *political* resistances in the sense, for example, of nations wishing to expand their populations for various purposes which they may consider to be entirely desirable or political, in the sense of governments simply assuming that a policy to reduce population increase or develop family planning would make it very difficult for them to sustain their political position; *cultural* resistances such as those concerned with norms of behavior in various groups, or those which result from cultural definitions of manhood or womanhood, on what is expected and reinforced through group pressures, on what gives people a sense of security; *religious* resistances—and the illustrations here have abounded—the Catholic world, the Moslem world, the Orthodox Jewish world, etc.; *psychological* resistances in the sense, for example, of evoking uncomfortable new ways of considering human sexuality and the difficulties on an individual basis in accepting these approaches whether related to cultural norms, religious norms, or other factors.

Many, but not all, at the Conference reflected the sense that one of the key functions of social work is to accept the mission of family planning and, to the extent national policy can be affected, a policy of restriction of population growth. The mission would include defining and overcoming the bases for resistances, without necessarily assuming that all of these resistances lack validity. In these areas, the cultural and psychological resistances, rather than the political and religious, appeared most germane to approaches based on the knowledge and skills of social work. It seemed an unduly extravagant expectation that social work could make much of a dent by itself, or even in company with other professions, on the political or religious areas. This does not at all mean that they should be ignored as sources of opposition that need to be overcome, but rather that they should be viewed as having lower priority as possible targets for change by the social work profession as such.

Repeatedly, both in the plenary sessions and in the discussion groups and certainly in the literature, the accent on reducing fatalism as a basic way of viewing the world was addressed. The belief in the capacity to affect one's destiny is a precondition, on an individual and collective basis, to being able to utilize family planning, conception control, and fertility control. In this respect, the reduction of fatalism as a view of one's relationship to the world is part and parcel of a developmental function, particularly for countries which are moving toward modernization. The social worker has a key role to play in this direction, to help harness the efforts toward instilling the will and the capacity to change this view, and, indeed, to help populations cope with the inevitable frustrations and strains attendant on developing a non-fatalist view of the world. Reference was made throughout the Conference to the necessity for the social worker to advocate necessary social change and to be constantly aware of the consequences of change. This theme was expressed in discussion of the social worker's support, for example, of movements which aim toward the greater dignity and rights of women. In effect, the utilization of family planning is a consequence of economic and social development, in nations as a whole and in sub-groups within nations. The change of view in man's capacity to affect his way of life and condition of life is a necessary component of such development.

We have noted in the United States and elsewhere a failure in the environmental area to anticipate and build in correctives to the harmful processes of technological change and a failure to make sufficient investment in analyzing the range of results that are likely to come from technological change—change which we would want in any event even if some results of such developments are harmful. The mass production of automobiles would not have been stopped because of anticipation of pollution of the atmosphere or wide-range effects on the sexual life and freedom of young adults. Nevertheless, it would have been useful to have had, with the production of the automobile, a concomitant investment, however modest, in considering the cultural as well as the material consequences of this technological innovation.

With respect to our particular subject matter, the scientific and technological break-throughs of the scope described as pending developments in conception control and fertility control will themselves undoubtedly give rise to a whole range of new problems. One may raise the question, therefore, of whether social work and all other professions and disciplines concerned with the social and human consequences of change ought not to begin considering the ramifications, beyond the desired and expected positive outcomes, of such developments as the once-a-month pill, temporary sterilization for men, the safely induced self-abortion, or even more dramatic prospects. Is this not the time to invest in the analysis of possible consequences and ways of coping with any that may be injurious to social and individual well-being?

It was suggested that social work would lose its function if all the children of the world were born wanted. There need be no fear. One of the few things that social workers, I think, have come to believe as a matter of faith is that there will always be a need for them. Even good things produce problems. With the developmental function of social work, moving on to a better quality of human life becomes part of a central responsibility, but there is no gainsaying the tremendous import of the observation that was made. The character of a great deal of what social work does, not only in the United States but internationally, would be markedly affected by a world in which all children were wanted.

We heard that with respect to family planning, in terms of the changes in this area, we have moved from an era in which it was considered immoral to an era in which it was considered positive for medical reasons to an era which we are now entering where it is a matter of human right and, perhaps, as has been suggested, to an era not too long away in which it might be a matter of social obligation. For many at the Conference, human right seemed the place to stop. Among social workers there is not altogether a readiness as yet to consider family planning as a social obligation. This may seem to some a culture lag or, among social workers themselves, a value lag.

To repeat, the note in relation to change that was perhaps the most striking referred to the responsibility that has to be located somewhere in the profession—if not among all those who are in social work. This responsibility is a major obligation to analyze the consequences of change for family life and for social organization and the ramifications of new concepts of human sexuality, particularly in the role of women, which are likely to emerge as the conception control and fertility control medical technology which has been discussed continues to expand.

Power

The second concept to which I referred was that of power. The key point in connection with the widespread utilization of family planning and population policy is that governmental authority is fundamental. Government has not only the power of setting national policy, devising legislation, and allocating funds, but also of affecting widespread cultural norms that set expectations, for example, on what is desirable in number of children. The voluntary sector can be most effective only as it is working together with the governmental sector. In many countries, of course, the voluntary sector has led the struggle toward change of legislation and demonstration of practice. By itself, however, the private sector cannot basically change a national picture. Government policy and authority and investment are essential for fundamental change.

A number of conference participants were concerned with "coercion" or "control" as a part of population policy, fearing that the exercise of such power might lead to abuse. The popular sensitivity about the term "control," as suggesting forceful coercion and so having a pejorative connotation, has evidently helped transform "birth control" into "family planning" and "population control" into "population policy." Yet, as the Conference discussion brought out, the kind of "control" generally reflected in the concept of population control is the use of incentives to reduce population growth through health education, public education affecting values, taxation policy, and other economic incentives. It was pointed out that the use of incentives and persuasion is an aspect of control in almost any government policy directed to the voluntary behavior of people, including, for example, policies to enhance their health or literacy. "Control" in this sense, directed to limiting population growth, is a different matter from completely restricting voluntary choice through, for example, treating a water supply to induce temporary infertility in the population.

The feeling was strong that, in respect to population policy, the direction of national measures for the control of population growth—including family planning—should begin with those that are voluntary, with incentives that are indirect. The prospect of deliberate constraints emerged as very difficult for most participants to accept. Instead, the hope was expressed that the changing of norms of individual conduct to conform to group and national interests would, in the terms used in our discussions, be made at the "micro-level" and thus obviate the necessity for nations to engage in official constraints at the "macro-level." It was also suggested that there was a measure of reality in the concept of social work power. While it could not appreciably affect world-wide population policy, it could have a distinct and direct effect on family planning, to the extent that family planning affects population policy.

The social work role is supportive of change toward a greater distribution of power, including the power to direct one's own life, in which family planning is one important aspect. Philip Hauser's reference to Durkheim on the cultural fact and the power of the cultural fact was cited.[1] The significance of this has not always been brought sufficiently to light. That there has been change in the way in which families have behaved in relation to reproduction is essentially due, as far as research can tell us, to a different set of cultural norms about expected, desirable behavior. How social work can move to reinforce a new cultural fact becomes important.

One final observation with respect to power has to do with the power of professional associations to state and advocate, to participate in population policy questions, even though they may not be the key bodies, and to have an input and a relation as well to the greater power of medicine. In this respect social work is not being urged to compete, but simply to have a chance to contribute to a much more total perspective and effort.

Values

It would be redundant and not particularly helpful to review all the references to values. This is a favorite expression, a favorite theme and exercise of social workers, and also extremely important. There are, however, a few observations with respect to values, as the subject was considered at the Conference, that should be singled out. One of the discussion groups made it quite clear that from their point of view the concept of

[1] Philip N. Hauser, "On Non-Family Planning Methods of Population Control" (mimeographed paper prepared for the International Conference on Family Planning, Dacca, Pakistan, January 28-February 4, 1969).

family well-being and family welfare is a higher value than population policy as far as social workers are concerned. The relationship would be, in this sense, similar to that of the counselor in a family agency in the United States who works with a couple about whether they should or should not separate or have a divorce, and whose concern lies with what is best for these two people and not necessarily with divorce policy in the United States. I am not suggesting that this is a fixed position, widely held, but simply reflecting the fact that not everyone in this field is really of the same mind or has the same set of premises. There is clearly a distinction being made by many with respect to commitments as between family welfare and population policy, as far as professional social work activity in family planning is concerned.

In a discussion of values, freedom and self-determination, of course, recur in constant refrain. Perhaps the most salient observations had to do with the notion that true freedom rests on knowledge and opportunity for options. Ignorance is not freedom. With respect to the poor in American society, it has been demonstrated over and over again that in the area of family planning they are proportionately less free than others. They have had a higher proportion of unwanted children and have had much less access to family planning facilities, approaches, and, particularly, to information. In other words, their opportunity for choice has been more restricted. The values with respect to freedom and self-determination also concern the necessity for social workers to have the means to help communities exercise their own judgment as to the policies and programs they want to have. Self-determination is not only seen on an individual level; public participation, consumer participation, and citizen participation are essential.

Health Professions and Social Work

Social work's relation to medicine and the health profession in this whole area came in for voluble and critical examination. The generalization that can be evoked is that social work is best able to contribute in the family planning area where the perspective of medicine itself is interprofessional and not restrictive. The observation was made that family planning has in some places, including the United States, been too clinical in its orientation to total target populations of would-be mothers. The concepts ought to affect the entire population through educational systems and through mass systems including the communication media. It was pointed out that, in order to prevent criminal abortion, prematurity, unwanted children, infant mortality, still-births, venereal disease, and so forth, a nation cannot have an adequate health policy without a family planning program. With this formulation practically everyone agreed, but there was a sense that this was not enough, that even this was too health-oriented, that there ought to be an even wider purview of the family planning concept, that not only health professions but many people have to participate. We must be mindful in the United States as well as elsewhere of rural areas as well as urban areas, of participation of social work in related professions in the rural areas as well as in the cities, since health concern with family planning tends to be so urban-dominated.

A leading medical authority at the Conference mentioned in one of the group discussion meetings that social workers themselves may become dispensers of contraceptives. If, for example, the pill that could be used once a month and is totally safe is available and can be issued without a prescription, it is perfectly possible one day for someone to see a social worker who would simply give the individual a pill and that would be that. The necessary relationship between the medical practitioner and family planning may be greatly reduced. In this sense the tie between social work and medicine is certainly affected by the technology and to a large extent by the administrative considerations in which social workers participate with doctors and others.

Knowledge and Competence

With respect to knowledge and competence, it is quite evident that social work has to draw from many sources. There is nothing new in this point, but it becomes increasingly vivid in this area of practice. Social work has to draw on medicine for contraceptive knowledge, on demography and economics for an understanding of population policy, on law for legislation and legal consideration, and on the broad field of social sciences for an understanding of the impact on the family, of strategies for attitudinal change, and for research approaches, but these knowledges all require translation for use in social work roles.

We need participation and research of many kinds, particularly into cultural norms, the understanding of anxieties and resistances in population groups, an understanding of differentials in population growth rates in various sub-cultures and why. The full use of university resources, especially for schools of social work located in universities, may be tapped for team-teaching and development of expertise in curriculum, field work opportunities, in-sevice training, staff development, and particularly continuing education for the enhancement of knowledge and competence.

One should note that the impact of the vast range of literature brought to our attention at this Conference has been considerable. While the flow of literature in this field may swamp us to the point that one gets simply submerged, it is important not only to know what is going on elsewhere, but to know the range of perspectives by which these problems are assessed.

Educational Approaches

I approach only briefly the main points relating to the role of social work education, in addition to those I have already indicated. There should be no great difficulty, however, for social work educators to fill in the specifics for the captions I will note, since they are experienced in such matters.

One approach for schools is direct action in the field of family planning, such as in the case of the school of social work in Teheran, Iran, which pioneered in establishing family planning clinics and programs. Schools can be drawn in to help prepare legislation and stimulate interest and joint action in other professional schools. In teaching social policy and social problems, population material could be part of the basic, on-going content to be studied. Such policy questions could also be related to income maintenance policies to see whether they reinforce or contradict one another.

Reference was repeatedly made to the necessity of preparing and utilizing indigenous workers and aides. Processes of developing community leadership and organization could, it was noted, take into account leadership and organization for family planning.

Population and family planning problems and materials could well offer content for use in the teaching of research and in preparing students to find and analyze data. Similarly, this content could be incorporated in training for supervision, administration, and consultation. At the same time, awareness of the issue of efficient utilization of manpower in the family planning field was stressed for social work training institutions as they prepare personnel to occupy diverse roles. The observation was made in this connection that the principle of conserving scarce manpower was important to other professions related to family planning, including medicine. It was noted by a representative of a developing country, that, in addition to the need for more effective use of paramedical personnel, doctors sometimes assume administrative positions which do not make the best use of their competence and for which their training has not necessarily prepared them.

Finally, it was stressed that the educational functions related to family planning and population policy in social work should be most heavily geared to the preventive, developmental functions. The relationship to individuals and individual families remains important, but not necessarily as a matter of high per capita investment across the population, especially in the poorer countries of the world. The issue of prevention, though, may mean a differentiation in priorities of manpower investment and a concentration of individualization on high risk groups.

CONCLUDING NOTE

This sketch of issues and problems raised and approaches to their solution stimulated by the Conference hardly does justice to the wealth of information and ideas to which the participants were exposed and with which they attempted to grapple. The net effect was a tremendous impetus to move social work education to preparing practitioners, researchers, administrators, planners, and policy analysts to be engaged more centrally and effectively in family planning and population policy. The fundamental importance of economy of means and time in so doing, of becoming more related to all other groups—including professions, disciplines, agencies, and citizen groups—in these efforts was underlined, with strong emphasis on staff in-service training and continuing education, as well as utilizing and enriching basic curriculum to the fullest.

The way was cleared for future developments of a more technical nature, related to the specific needs and interests of different regions and countries and schools. All national representatives learned once more how much it is possible to learn from one another, as well as from various disciplines and professions, and that distinctions in the level of economic development are not necessarily related to the level of expertise in population policy or family planning. It was repeatedly noted with reference to social work education, for example, how far the United States lags behind other countries in the field of family planning. More important, the recognition remained strong that this is a world-wide issue, and social work education should move fast and vigorously in order to help the field of social work make its most effective contribution.

Social Work Discovers A New Responsibility

AN ANALYTIC REPORT:
IRWIN T. SANDERS

INTRODUCTION

Social workers, particularly in the Western world, have been little concerned with population policy or with fertility control. The former, sometimes thought of as population control, relates to the whole complex of policies which affect the growth and composition of a population. These policies can range from welfare measures encouraging or discouraging large families to steps to reduce infant mortality. Legislators, planners of many sorts, economists, demographers, and a wide variety of other professionals are all involved in some aspects of population policy without necessarily using the term.

Fertility control, as only a part of population policy is more limited in scope. Since its stress has traditionally been upon methods of birth control and family planning, its development has been directed primarily by medical and public health personnel.

Today, however, social workers are asking themselves some pointed questions. Are they as a profession contributing their expertise sufficiently to the population problems besetting mankind? If not, in what ways can they participate in social planning which aims to improve the health, educational, and social status of the individual family and, in turn, advance the welfare of society as a whole? Is the time ripe for a convergence of social work skills with those of other professions already dealing with population problems?

Irwin T. Sanders is chairman of the Department of Sociology, Boston University.

To test the timeliness of this convergence and to indicate possible implementations, an International Conference on Social Work Education, Population, and Family Planning was held in the East-West Center, University of Hawaii, in March, 1970. Those attending represented 28 countries from all of the continents as well as a cross-section of social work educators, demographers, directors of family planning programs, medical and public health professionals, and some social scientists. Funds were provided by the Agency for International Development to the Council on Social Work Education, which worked in cooperation with the East-West Center, to achieve this exchange of ideas and experience.

Background material for the main themes of the Conference included: (1) the social worker's belated interest in population questions, (2) the dimensions of the "population problems," and (3) the world-wide system of social work education which has the responsibility for preparing social workers for effective service in population and family planning programs. A sketch of these three factors follows.

The Social Worker's Belated Interest

On what basis does the social worker profess a belated interest in the efforts made, particularly since 1963, to halt the runaway populations predicted for certain parts of the world? The Hawaii Conference has documented much of this, as indicated in later sections of this report, but such documentation is of very recent vintage.

The top-level social welfare policymakers from 96 nations, who met as recently as 1968 at the first United Nations Conference of Ministers Responsible for Social Welfare, say almost nothing about population policy or family planning—at least as reported in a summary of their deliberations on the training of social welfare personnel. There are two or three references to the need for research in demography and one single suggestion that social workers should be "introduced" to techniques of family planning along with such other topics as personality development and the special problems of the aged.[1]

On the other hand, in contrast to many other social welfare documents which indicate relationships between social work and population problems, two slender reports of earlier institutes connecting the two were available

---

[1] Council on Social Work Education (published for International Association of Schools of Social Work and International Council on Social Welfare), *The Essential Task: Training Social Welfare Manpower* (New York: CSWE, 1969).

to conference participants,[2] as was the policy statement adopted in 1967 by the National Association of Social Workers of the United States. These publications are strong on what ought to be done; they are very weak on what has been done by social workers in the United States in this field. In fact, one U.S. participant at the Hawaii Conference observed:

> I am primarily aware of social work's uninvolvement in population and family planning services. While it is true that public welfare agencies, often directed and staffed by social workers, have been involved in funding and, to a lesser extent, promoting family planning services or initiating policy discussions, I know of no reliable measurement or appraisal of the current involvement of the profession, or the quality of that involvement.

Participants from countries in different geographical areas of the world, while recognizing the desirability of social work involvement, pointed out how minimal this had been:

Argentina: In Argentina very little has been done on family planning services. There are no official operating programs in this field. Only in the largest cities such as Buenos Aires and Córdoba, some isolated programs exist as part of the work of hospitals, medical clinics, etc.

The Schools of Social Work do not include specially this subject area in their curricula and social workers do not pay much attention to it.

In Argentina, the population rate is declining and this fact explains, in part, the situation.

Indonesia: Modern social work and social work education are at the very beginning stage of development in Indonesia. Therefore, no direct contributions have been made by social work so far to family planning services, research, or training of family planning personnel.

Japan: I do not think that social work has contributed very much to the education or training programs related to family planning in Japan although the idea of family planning is very popular and it is practised very commonly among the general public.

Uganda: The current pattern of social services in Uganda is that the Uganda Government is the largest provider and promoter of the social welfare services. The Uganda Government neither promotes nor discourages family planning. A voluntary organization, the Uganda Family Planning Association, provides a limited family planning service. Therefore, the social welfare education contribution to family planning is minimal.

---

[2] Florence Haselkorn, ed., *Family Planning: The Role of Social Work, Perspectives in Social Work,* Vol. II, No. 1 (Garden City, N.Y.: Adelphi University School of Social Work, 1968).

Alice M. Varela, ed., *Family Planning,* based on the 1968 Annual Institute for Social Workers in Health, Education, and Welfare in New Jersey (New Brunswick, N.J.: The Graduate School of Social Work, Rutgers—The State University, 1968).

The family planning literature does not devote much space to social work participation. A book entitled *Family Planning Programs: An International Survey* makes a few references to social welfare or social work, but it does not picture any roles for social workers in program planning or program direction.[3] In fact, one publication summarizing characteristics of 20 national family planning programs lists only one program which specifies social workers as among the personnel to be employed.[4] Such professional compartmentalization of activities is, of course, not uncommon, but given the magnitude of the problems being tackled one might well wonder whether the walls between the professional fields can any longer be justified. One physician active in family planning said at the Conference: "Before I came here I had never thought about any possible social work participation, but now I can see that social workers have much to contribute."

Despite the negative evidence, some Conference participants report what might be termed, at best, a modest involvement in family planning programs:

Brazil: There are no national programs on population and family planning as such. Only local agencies in the largest cities, the majority of which belong to the "Sociedade de Bem-Estar Familiar, BEMFAM," founded in 1965 under the auspices of the "XIV Brazilian Institute of Gynaecology and Obstetrics," have a few social workers on their staff. In many family welfare agencies, family planning is one of the aspects of social treatment through group discussion or individual interviews, with proper referral to agencies with family planning services.

Canada: Three years ago, Montreal's social work agencies started the *Centre de planification familiale,* with three main functions: (a) to make studies; (b) to train social workers; and (c) to see how social agencies of the province could help their cases in family planning.

This Centre is in correspondence with all the social work agencies of the province; it offers a training program of 120 hours in family planning, which is given in 12 different cities of the province during two years.

Nevertheless, the schools of social work are reluctant to offer courses in family planning.

Colombia: Social workers are not involved in policy development or establishment of family planning services at a national or regional

[3] Bernard Berelson, ed., *Family Planning Programs: An International Survey* (New York: Basic Books, 1969).

[4] Dorothy Nortman, "Population and Family Planning Programs: A Factbook," *Reports on Population/Family Planning* (New York: Population Council and the International Institute for the Study of Human Reproduction, Columbia University, December, 1969).

level. They do participate in local and agency levels, especially in private programs.

Although they have not participated in designing the research, some social workers have helped in research which identifies attitudes toward family planning.

Where the social worker is part of interdisciplinary programs of popular education, she usually plays the role of a paraprofessional and does not contribute as a team member with a professional status.

The Philippines: Few Filipino social workers with professional training are presently active in family planning. The handful now engaged are used primarily in the campaign to remove blocks and resistance to the acceptance of family planning. Some are also active in the areas of policy making, information, education, and in provision of services. Some social work educators involved in the above areas have started to introduce family planning in some core courses in social work training at the university level, e.g., in courses such as social policy and community organization. Recently the Department of Social Welfare has included family planning in the pre-service training of all its new field workers.

Thailand: The Bangkok Municipality has 22 health centers, each of which is supposed to have one social worker as well as two public health nurses along with the doctors, dentists, dental hygienist, six graduate nurses, and auxiliary workers. The public health nurses and social workers are charged with similar responsibilities.

In some countries there is evidence of a more significant involvement of the social work profession in family planning activities:

Hong Kong: The Family Planning Association of Hong Kong has a Social Work Section which is closely co-ordinated with the Clinic Section, Research Section, and Publicity Section. This Social Work Section is beginning to redirect its performance toward a social work approach. Instead of the emphasis upon quantity of contacts they now are following one-to-one or small group interviews.

Forty-six welfare workers are employed by the Association. All new workers have to go through an orientation course which lasts for four weeks.

Iran: The Teheran School of Social Work was established in 1958. At that time, it was realized that its long-range goals for the welfare of the people could not be fully achieved unless family planning was included among its services for the families of especially low income. Therefore, a group of volunteers including students, social workers, faculty members, medical and paramedical friends joined together and started a family planning clinic service for needy women. This volunteer group later was organized and formed the Family Planning Association of Iran. Thus this Association was established and began to function several years before family planning was made a national policy by the government in 1967. Meanwhile subjects relating to family planning were included in the curriculum of the Teheran School of Social Work, physiology of reproduction, health and sex education for the first year, family planning methods and its importance and demography for the second and third year, population and its relations to social and economical planning for the fourth year. Field instruction in the area of population studies and family planning was also organized for the students. Research on the above subject and a great deal of literature such as posters, handbooks, and educational materials on family planning have also been published by the School.

The Director of the School was elected Chairman of the Family Planning Association of Iran, thus keeping family planning well integrated into the family and community welfare services. The School and the Association are at the moment together launching a nationwide programme on sex and family life education.

Jamaica: Family planning in Jamaica was pioneered by voluntary social workers and non-governmental welfare agencies. The Jamaica Family Planning Association is very active and is administered on the parish level by committees on which social workers are represented.

The government has set up The National Family Planning Board, a statutory body to intensify family planning activities; strengthen and develop areas of contraception and medical service, cytology, education and training, research and evaluation; and to provide the personnel services.

The National Family Planning Board has drawn on the expertise of social workers (including community development workers) both at the policy-making and administrative levels. The Board works in close co-operation with both statutory and voluntary social work agencies.

Pakistan: A survey in 1956 revealed that only 4% of the Family Planning Officers were M.A.s in Social Work. It is now recognized that the success of the program depends upon the effectiveness of the front-line worker who establishes and maintains contact with the client and is capable of maintaining client participation. It is now believed that the program should be measured in terms of attitudinal and behavioral changes relative to family planning methods and practice. Therefore, training of workers in the techniques of social work methods, particularly taking account of the Community Development approach, has received wide acceptance among planners, policy makers, and voluntary workers.

The cases cited here are not sufficient to permit any sound generalizations about the conditions underlying the entry of social work into family planning. It does seem clear, however, that where it originated the program, as in Jamaica and Iran, social work has remained influential; where it is viewed as a paraprofessional field to muster clients for the clinics or even to make follow-up visits after clients attend the clinics, social workers consider their role unsatisfactory. In those countries, where social workers have been involved in both research and training in family planning programs, as in the case of India, they begin to contribute some professional competence. Full advantage of the situation will not have been taken, however, until social workers participate in the policy and administrative decisions of the programs with which they are connected. How possible this is in certain countries, and under what conditions, remains to be explored. It also suggests an analysis of how a crescive, or rising, profession such as social work develops colleague relations with an established profession such as medicine.

The Urgent Population Situation

Anyone who was not a social worker might well have asked himself at the Hawaii Conference just why social workers were worried about being so effectively left out of family planning programs or their failure to provide the leadership which might have been expected of them. Are they just trying to make new jobs for themselves? Conversations at the Conference quickly dispelled any ideas about self-serving motivation. The social workers there, like other professionals in many parts of the world, had become deeply concerned about the population problems confronting mankind; they had begun to see that a quantitative approach to human fertility taken by certain types of specialists left out of the picture the humane considerations embodied in a nation's values; they also observed that the quality of human life—a primary social work concern—would suffer if numbers outran the ability of a society to provide the needs of its people. Also, there was a gnawing sense of guilt that social work had come into the act so late, that its practitioners—at least those with a master's degree—were too often not in position to contribute to social policy in this area or even to provide an acknowledged professional service.

The sense of urgency which social workers began to share with their fellow conferees, some of whom had worked on "birth-control" in the pioneering era with Margaret Sanger, was reinforced by the packets of materials selected following a critical survey of publications useful for social work. These came from such organizations as the Population Council, the International Planned Parenthood Federation, the United Nations, and other governmental and non-governmental agencies associated with population and family planning activities. The materials were distributed for study prior to the Conference.

The address by Milos Macura, director of the Population Division of the United Nations, particularly dramatized the situation. After explaining the origin of the population problem, he reminded the Conference that the first doubling of population since 1750 took about 150 years, the second about 65 years, and the third may not take more than 35 years. In 1965 the world's population was placed at about 3,280 million and by the year 2000 it may reach 6,500 million. While it is estimated that the developed countries will experience a rate of growth of one percent per annum over the next 15 years, the developing countries are expected to have a rate growth of about 2.4 percent per annum.

This means that between 1970 and 1985 the following provisions will have to be made just to take care of additional population with nothing included for improving the low standard of living in many parts of the world:

1. Food, housing, clothing, and other essentials for 1,117 million additional people (or 44 percent more in 1985 than in 1970) in the less developed regions and 184 million people of working age (or 17 percent more) in the more developed regions;
2. Employment in order to utilize the productive capacity of an additional 660 million people of working age (47 percent more) in the less developed regions, and 115 million in the more developed ones (17 percent more);
3. Improvement of prospects and opportunities for 217 million additional youth (or 45 percent more than in the more developed ones);
4. Basic education for an additional school-age population of 273 million (43 percent more) in the less developed and 20 million (or 10 percent) in the more developed regions;
5. Child care for 131 million new young children (32 percent) in the less developed regions, and 22 million (24 percent) in the more developed ones;
6. Security and protection for a significant percentage of 53 million people aged 65 years and over in the less developed regions (an increase of 63 percent) and 27 million people in the more developed regions (26 percent increase);
7. Education and services needed to control pregnancy and birth for 248 million more women of reproductive age (46 percent more than in 1970) in the less developed regions, and for a portion of 31 million women in the more developed regions;
8. Space and facilities needed for an additional 537 million urban population (84 percent more) in the less developed regions and for 258 million (or 36 percent) in the more developed regions;
9. Agricultural land, employment, and housing for a new rural

population of 549 million (or 30 percent increase) in the less developed regions.[5]

Dr. Macura cites, therefore, as the most crucial factor in the demographic consideration of the world the need to lower population growth and its annual increments. Otherwise, with scarce natural resources and capital, it will be difficult to satisfy all kinds of requirements which people are being taught to expect. He did not need to use scare tactics to convince an already convinced group; the implications of his statistics for governmental policy and social welfare programs proved sobering enough.

The World-Wide System of Social Work Education

There was ready recognition that schools of social work had not done and were not now doing enough to prepare social workers for a full-fledged role in family planning programs. What is a school of social work? What is its program? How do such schools differ in various countries? These were questions that experts from the health field and the social sciences and demographers needed to have answered if they were to counsel on ways to improve social work education.

Katherine A. Kendall, director of International Education of the Council on Social Work Education and secretary-general of the International Association of Schools of Social Work, had anticipated these questions in her Conference paper.[6] After showing how social work as a professional discipline had its origins in the personal and religious charity, mutual aid, social reform, and social action movements of the nineteenth century, she went on to explain why and where schools of social work were set up. The first full-scale school of social work in the world was established in Amsterdam in 1899, to be followed by a school in London in 1903 and in New York in 1904. Approximately 300 schools of social work were in operation in 42 countries in 1950 when the United Nations made its first international survey of training for social work. Of the 300 schools, 204 in 24 countries were members of the International Association of Schools of Social Work. In 1970, more than 400 schools in 52 countries belong to the International Association. Once, therefore, the social work profession decides what it wants to do in population programs and family planning, there is a world-wide training apparatus which can respond to the need. Each school will, of course, work out its own pro-

[5] Milos Macura, "A World-wide View of a Universal Problem," *supra*, pp. 69-81.

[6] Katherine A. Kendall, "Systems of Social Work Education: A World View," *supra*, pp. 115-123.

gram in keeping with its own political and cultural approach to social problems.

Established both within and outside of universities, schools of social work are organized at varying levels of education: post-graduate, graduate, undergraduate, technical, or secondary. Completion of a program of social work education may lead to a degree, diploma, or certificate or to the title of social worker. In North America and in a growing number of countries of Asia, there are schools operating at the level of graduate university education and offering a two-year program leading to a master's degree. Undergraduate university education is the basic qualifying route for professional social work in New Zealand and Australia, much of Asia, and most of Latin America. There are also undergraduate programs in the Middle East and in a growing number of countries in Africa. Professional preparation, usually at the level of undergraduate education but in non-university schools of social work, is characteristic of the European continent, some countries of Africa, and a few countries of Latin America.

The implications of this picture of wide diversity are that social workers in various countries are prepared for different levels of participation in family planning programs. Where their training has been at the secondary or post-secondary level, they should expect to serve as "field workers" or as members of teams including other personnel equivalent in educational background. On the other hand, where the social worker has received full university preparation or post-graduate training his aspirations point to the higher reaches of policymaking and program direction.

The theoretical content of social work curricula may be described as embracing: (1) study of man, his biological, intellectual, emotional endowment and functioning and the social and cultural factors affecting his development; (2) study of society, its organizations and institutions, social and economic problems, social change and development; and (3) study of social work theory and practice. Much of the foundation knowledge comes from the social and behavioral sciences and allied professions but social work is increasingly concerned with the development of its own theoretical body of knowledge. New educational trends, new combinations of theory and practice, and ways of viewing the social role of social work are reflected in the adaptation of curriculum any school makes from year to year.

The core of professional education for social work is often thought to be field practice. This initiates the students under supervision in the actual relationships with clients, whether by helping individuals and families through the casework approach, or in working with groups, or by helping communities organize their resources for social ends.

New targets for social work in many countries now include greater emphasis in theoretical instruction and field practice on the prevention of social problems, creation of equal opportunity for all citizens, mobilization of disadvantaged groups to effect change, the re-structuring of environmental forces and institutions, implementation of planned social change, and active professional involvement with large population groups. The social worker, in these contexts, is seen as an agent of social change and a key contributor to social development. His professional methodology may employ a range of interventive, developmental, action-oriented, and advocacy techniques that often build upon but frequently extend far beyond the characteristic approaches of casework, group work, and community organization. In addition, social policy formulation, social welfare administration, social planning, and social work research increasingly come to the fore as recognized methods of professional social work practice taught by some, if not all, schools of social work.

Common to all schools of social work is concern for the disadvantaged, which constitutes an important group to which family planning programs seek to give the same opportunities as more privileged groups which have had more ready access to family planning information and facilities.

The majority of the social work representatives at the Hawaii Conference held full professional qualifications from schools of social work, which meant that they had completed the social work education available in their countries. They also had considerable experience in several facets of their profession. One sensed, in talking with them, that they felt part of a world-wide professional network though their cultural backgrounds were as diverse as each of the continents. A common educational core of social work courses plus the practice of working in social welfare agencies of many kinds made them feel they shared a similar professional outlook. Thus the Conference was a search not so much for tasks that an individual might do in family planning, nor merely what a school of social work could do, but rather a search for what the profession of social work itself should be doing and how these goals for practice could be related to the educational aspirations for the social work students of the future.

IDENTIFYING THE SOCIAL WORK CONTRIBUTION TO PROGRAM FORMULATION

The success of any action program is directly related to the quality of thought used in its formulation. At the Hawaii Conference social workers pointed out that many of their number—particularly those in the community organization field—had acquired an expertise in action programs which could be applied to population and family planning programs. Many, too, with experience in preparing and furthering the enactment of social legislation of many kinds were aware of the political process within which government programs must operate. In order to see what unique contributions social workers might make to the development of population or family planning programs as a specific type, one must first have a picture of the nature of these programs. They are of two general kinds: the government-sponsored program and the voluntary program. Each will be considered in turn, then attention will be paid to the social and cultural factors which affect popular attitudes toward such programs. After considering all these factors, it is possible to assess the social work contribution to the various programs.

National Population Programs

"There is not one single government among the family of about 130 sovereign nations which has not established a policy aimed at improving health conditions, extending longevity and combating mortality," according to Dr. Macura.[7] He adds that of these 130 governments only 30 have adopted policies designed to moderate family size and composition, rationalize and humanize reproduction, and moderate fertility. "It is surprising but true," he notes, "that the two respective policies, both of which affect family size and population growth, were not pursued simultaneously until 1951, when India upgraded the idea of fertility control to a government policy level." Government policies differ in their demographic objectives and motives. Many governments organize family planning services in order to moderate fertility and population growth, but others have no demographic targets and a few even favor a larger population.

Governments become involved in national population programs for different reasons in the opinion of Alan Guttmacher.[8] First, there is the economic reason. For example, in a country such as Botswana, which Guttmacher had visited as a consultant, the government hoped that a family planning program would help curtail population growth to the point of improving the economic picture, allowing greater industrialization, and reducing unemployment by cutting the annual inflow of youths into the labor pool. The main medical reason for a government program of effective contraception is the reduction of illegal abortion, "a world endemic disease," according to Dr. Guttmacher, perhaps second to none in mortality and morbidity. A third reason is that some governments

[7] Macura, *op cit.*

[8] Alan F. Guttmacher, "Leadership Perspectives: Governmental and Voluntary," *supra,* pp. 97-103.

have become interested in popularizing birth control as a basic human right for their people. Ability to have babies by *choice* rather than by *chance* should not be the right of only one segment of the population; it must be a privilege shared by all.

One Conference discussion group made four specific recommendations about national programs, thus reflecting the importance attached to them:

> 1. The present rates of population growth constitute such a serious threat to individual fulfillment, the quality of family life, and social development that all nations should be urged to adopt and implement national family planning policies if they have not already done so.
>
> 2. The rates of population growth constitute such a severe threat to human freedom that all professionals should be urged to collaborate in widespread educational efforts, formal and informal, to alert people to the facts, their meanings, and their urgent implications for the entire world.
>
> 3. Wherever family planning programs, incentives toward voluntary family limitation, or coercive measures are in use, the particular concern of social workers will be to protect families from discriminatory treatment.
>
> 4. Social workers should promote development of national family planning policies, explicating the national goals for all families, to serve as a frame of reference against which all present provisions and future proposals impinging on family welfare can be measured.

The workshop, after stating these recommendations, refused to spell out the ABC's of what a national program should be, since the members believed that national policy should reflect the culture and the history of each of the nations. Yet, one does need to get down to some program specifics if definite suggestions about social work participation are to be made.

S. M. Keeny deals with the problem of getting a national program started. He notes:

> To mobilize a *national* program is basically a simple job. Money, staff, supplies, and a clear-cut organization are necessary. Wherever possible, the program should relate to mother and child welfare in the public health system, but it should not wait for these services if they do not exist.[9]

---

[9] S. M. Keeny, "Family-Planning Programs: What They Cost and How They Work," in Berelson, *Family Planning Programs . . .*, pp. 215-216.

He thinks the steps of organization are relatively few. The seven listed are familiar to anyone connected with community organization or community development:

1. Getting the program accredited [by which he means accepted by the leaders and public].
2. Estimating the cost and obtaining the money.
3. Fixing tentative targets.
4. Hiring and training the staff.
5. Getting supplies and equipment into place.
6. Estimating the minimum necessary organization to do the job.
7. *Getting started* promptly—the moment staff are ready anywhere.[10]

Each of these points deserves extended treatment but reference will be made to them again in describing how social workers can actually fit into the fromulation of programs. Lest Mr. Keeny's observations make the task of program development seem too simple, one should remember —as Bernard Berelson has pointed out—that any program must recognize that people's perceptions of consquences will determine what is scientifically available, politically acceptable, administratively feasible, economically justifiable, and morally tolerated. He regrets that there still does not exist the informed, firm, and constant conviction in high circles that the population problem is a matter with truly great ramifications for human welfare.[11]

Along with the conviction about the seriousness of the problem and a commitment to its solution, a government must work closely with its citizens in the development of policies affecting the population problem. Antonio Ordoñez-Plaja stressed this repeatedly in his Conference paper. He sees decision-making as based on interchange of concepts between the governors and the governed, a product of the knowledge of the problem and its repercussions. Social workers can collaborate on governmental population policies in such a way as to avoid conflicts, but all decision-making must be preceded by sufficiently ample and objective information.[12]

Those attending the Conference had numerous opportunities to think concretely about specific national programs which were described by participants familiar with them. For example, there was much useful material about the family planning program of India, with especially

---

[10] *Ibid.*, p. 216.

[11] Bernard Berelson, *Beyond Family Planning* (New York: The Population Council, Studies in Family Planning Number 38, February, 1969), pp. 12-13.

[12] Antonio Ordoñez-Plaja, "Perspectives on National Approaches: Government and the People," *supra*, pp. 92-96.

appropriate references from the *Social Work Forum,* the journal of the Indian Association of Trained Social Workers, which devoted one issue entirely to social workers and family planning (Vol. IV, No. 4, October, 1966). India has a high priority government-sponsored program of family planning, with a separate Department of Family Planning at the central government level. In the states there is a separate unit in the Directorate of Public Health. At the block and district levels, community education or extension education workers are used and not social work personnel. At the field service level, "social workers" are used, but these are not graduates of the masters' degree programs. Professional social workers are often employed, however, in short-term training programs for family planning program personnel and also in research positions at the state and central government levels.

More and more governments, one can safely assume, will move more actively into national programs relating to population policy. How these are planned, what goals are set, what kind of organizational approach is used, and what data are used in making allocations of material and personnel—these and many other considerations are of deep interest to professional people in social welfare.

Voluntary Programs

Though the national programs described above are at times massive, spectacular, and altogether necessary for rapid results, voluntary programs have pioneered in the field and have provided both the climate of opinion and many of the organizational and clinical techniques on which national programs are based. Dr. Guttmacher's Conference paper traced the history of modern birth control efforts, pointing out how Margaret Sanger, in 1916, opened in Brownsville, a slum area of Brooklyn, New York, the first birth control clinic outside of Holland. Despite being jailed eight times she was able to begin and move forward the world birth control movement, basing it at first in non-governmental, special voluntary agencies.

Today the Planned Parenthood Federation of America, a lineal descendant of the National Birth Control League started by Margaret Sanger, operates 525 clinics in 135 cities and serves 350,000 patients each year. The International Planned Parenthood Federation, founded by eight nations in Bombay in 1952, now operates with an annual budget of 10.5 million dollars and counts 66 nations as members.[13]

One Conference participant told about the introduction of family plan-

---

[13] Guttmacher, *op. cit.*

ning into Jamaica in the 1930s by an Englishwoman who came to the island at the invitation of a voluntary social worker and gave a series of lectures under the auspices of the Jamaica Welfare Ltd.—a non-governmental community development agency. This led to the formation of the Birth Control League which later merged with another voluntary agency—the Jamaica Family Planning Association—which was organized in a rural area. The program of this agency, still very active in the field, includes the operation of family planning clinics, family planning education, and motivation carried out through a staff of family planning educators and encouragement visitors. The latter are village-level workers who, after receiving some elementary training, work directly with individuals and families. The Association estimates that approximately 55 percent of the persons attending family planning clinics have been alerted to the opportunities by the encouragement visitors. The Association has recently launched an educational program directed toward men. In the view of the reporter from Jamaica, the pioneer work of these organizations and the efforts of other social welfare agencies and service clubs in educating public opinion influenced the decision of the government to formulate a national family planning policy and to launch a national family planning program financed by government funds.

One could cite country after country where concerned people began in a private, voluntary way to help mothers control the number and spacing of their children. Now, on an increasing scale, governments are giving financial support to private associations. This is particularly true where a national program does not exist, but such support usually continues where there also are national programs. The concept of teamwork between the public and private agencies seems especially appropriate in the population and family planning fields. Some of the countries where public funds go to voluntary associations are Mauritius, Nigeria, Southern Rhodesia, Barbados, Brazil, Eduador, Mexico, Puerto Rico, South Korea, Indonesia, and Malaysia.[14]

In a country such as India, despite a highly developed government program, the voluntary sector still has a role to play. Avabai B. Wadia, president of the Family Planning Association of India, Bombay, explains what this is:

> In a democratic society in transition such as ours, voluntary effort runs the whole gamut from charitable and ameliorative measures to welfare, and to community services. Its unique value lies in its catalytic effect in an otherwise stagnant situation. The impetus for change, reconstruction, and a conscious striving for a better future has to come ultimately from the people at large, but they, in turn,

[14] Nortman, *op. cit.*, pp. 32-37.

depend upon those who are acknowledged to be the social innovators, to show the way.

Thus true voluntary service keeps in tune with the people and yet is one step ahead—anticipating and guiding people's needs on a rising plane of achievements—material, emotional, and of spirit.

For this very reason, our national government has actively sought to encourage, assist, and increase the scope of voluntary effort in the country, and this has led to a tremendous expansion of voluntary work.[15]

The important role that voluntary organizations can play in communication and motivation aspects of family planning and also in undertaking certain types of training, setting up service facilities where feasible, and, in some cases, undertaking field research has been indicated. Voluntary associations do, however, need some professional leaders who can help forge a new link between themselves and the unpaid volunteer. Such agencies need a structure suited to their purpose, with a different kind suggested for groups with a general membership to promote the formation of public opinion than for those which have to administer projects or day-to-day activities. The latter requires managerial skills which volunteer or lay officials and workers may not possess. According to Mrs. Wadia, voluntary associations depending heavily on government finance must be on guard to be sure that they do not become stereotyped, officialized, and depersonalized.

Certainly aiding positive interaction between the public and private sector of welfare is a function of many social workers. Its existence should hold no mystery for them.

Attitudes and Values Concerning Population Policies

In formulating population and family planning programs account has to be taken of the possible cultural and psychological resistances the programs might encounter. This topic was treated in considerable detail in the Conference paper by Selo Soemardjan.[16] The major points stressed in his paper, with illustrations from his own country (Indonesia), were also alluded to by other participants. There was clear recognition that one needs to distinguish between the attitudes and values of those *officials* who decide whether or not such programs are to be established and, if so, how much attention they will receive, and the *general public* for whom

[15] Avabai Wadia, "The Role of Voluntary Organizations in the Family Planning Programme," *Social Work Forum,* Vol. IV, No. 4 (October, 1966), pp. 33-36.

[16] Selo Soemardjan, "Social Attitudes Toward Population Policies in Less Developed Societies," *supra,* pp. 104-114.

the programs are developed.

Not all officials are friendly to programs which reduce population growth. Australia and Ethiopia are considered underpopulated, according to representatives from those countries; Uganda also feels that it is not overpopulated. However, for most developing countries, it was agreed, the officials might be persuaded that a smaller population, with better educated citizens and a higher standard of living, will occur only if there is economic and social development. The argument that a country needs a larger population in order to have a bigger market for domestic products was held to be true only if the buying power of the people is going up rather than down, the latter being almost a sure consequence of excessive population growth. Political leaders are also sensitive to the electorate or clientele whom they serve and would want to be sure that population policies did not cut down on the number supporting them in favor of supporters for rivals.

The fact that every year more countries are giving support to population programs shows that the political leaders and administrative officials recognize the connection between controlled fertility and economic and social development.

The role of a charismatic leader in a developing country was seen as tremendously important in an effort to persuade people to change to new approaches to size of family, contraception, and family life.

The second party to the acceptance of a national policy or voluntary family planning program is the general public, the men and women whose individual decisions determine whether the policies are implemented or not. In one Conference discussion group, mention was made of the Davis and Blake study, which holds that three intermediate variables exist between elements in the social system and the resultant variable of fertility. These are: *factors affecting exposure to intercourse,* including such things as age of sexual unions and frequency of coitus; *factors affecting exposure to conception,* such as reliance upon sterilization or use of contraception; and *factors affecting gestation and successful parturition,* such as involuntary or voluntary fetal mortality.[17] In this connection, Dr. Macura suggested that along with birth control other alternatives be promoted: postponing the age of marriage, requiring that young women enter the labor force, improvment of education for all so that people could be expected to embrace a small-size family norm.

How sex is viewed in a society has much to do with the acceptance

---

[17] Kingsley Davis and Blake J. Davis, "Social Structure and Fertility: An Analytic Framework," *Economic Development and Social Change,* Vol. 4, No. 3 (April, 1956), pp. 211-235.

of family planning. Professor Soemardjan raised three questions which different societies and even different individuals within a society respond to in varied ways:

> Is sex information, which is the principal part of birth control, a private or public affair?
>
> Is reproduction a human act or is it an act of nature? If subject to human will, then it is legitimate and feasible for man to control it.
>
> Is reproduction an act of man, or is it predestined by God?[18]

A participant from Thailand described how shyness inhibits the discussion of sexual matters by women, especially young girls. They just ignore family planning programs.

Some thought that no religion could stand, for long, the challenges of man's progress if it failed to find an acceptable and effective solution for man's social problems. Religious norms become re-interpreted if they are in conflict with the real needs of a society. Yet, in Djakarta and its surrounding rural area in Indonesia religious reasons are given by 74 percent of the males and 71 percent of the females for their disapproval of birth control. Elsewhere, as Herman Stein noted in his Conference summary, fatalism as a basic way of viewing the world must change as a precondition if an individual is to utilize the family planning notion of conception and fertility control.[19] It was also pointed out that religious bodies, such as the Catholic Church, may accept some and not other approaches to family planning.

Ideas about children also seem to influence marital behavior. "Children, people argue, are an investment for old age. They are also a security factor against divorce. It is the duty of a legally married couple to raise a family with children who will continue to bear the family name."[20] In Hong Kong a survey showed that the sex of children of the family was an important factor in considering family limitation. Normally, according to a Conference participant from that city, the couple, whether high or low income, will not consider birth control until one or more sons have been born. Birth control seems acceptable if the family already has male offspring. A participant from India explained the past importance of the norm of a large family, which proved useful in meeting the manpower requirements of the joint family; it also provided social security in the form of a large number of future earners. The prevailing large-size family norm, therefore, has to be changed into a small-size family norm. For the Philippines it is clear that the "more children one has, the greater

---

[18] Soemardjan, *op. cit.*

[19] Herman Stein, "The Context of Social Work's Contribution," *supra,* pp. 11-22.

[20] Soemardjan, *op. cit.*

assurance that there will be some left should some die" is a logical conclusion for village people constantly seeing the ravages of disease and the helplessness of neighbors when malady strikes.[21]

Another variable related to acceptance of family planning is the type of customary interaction between spouses. "In Islamic societies birth control practice is legitimate only if approval by both marriage partners is given. But neither of the two is generally bold enough to start discussing the subject with the other. As a consequence no explicit approval of either spouse will ever be expressed and no actual practice carried out."[22] In many societies the male must give his permission before a wife can adopt any contraceptive practice, a fact which has led the critics of many family programs to suggest that more of the publicity and contact work be done with the men.

One could continue at much greater length to catalog the positive and negative aspects of culture which affect individual attitudes toward birth control. The words used—"family planning" or "responsible parenthood" instead of "birth control"—have turned out to be important. The fear on the part of minority groups in a country that they are particular targets for fertility control while other groups are not was mentioned by many participants as an obstacle to cooperation in family planning programs.

Public acceptance of family planning programs is connected, too, with the extent of literacy. Professor Soemardjan spoke of "filling the vacuum with knowledge." He sees a principal goal as getting the message through to the audience, but points out that people have culturally defined attitudes toward various types of media just as much as they have attitudes toward size of family. "Mass communication media and all available modern techniques of information distribution can be applied only in population sectors where literacy and the habit of reading and listening and watching mass media of communication have become institutionalized. In other illiterate groups of the population, information has to be channeled through recognized head men of village communities, tribes, and clans to lend it the authority of officialness."

The discussion of cultural and psychological obstacles brought participants the realization that the nature of these obstacles, while apparently much the same from country to country, are really quite different. Many participants remarked that points made in terms of Indonesia did not

---

[21] Nena R. Bustrillos, "Some Socio-Cultural Correlates in Family Planning in a Rural Area in the Philippines," mimeographed. For a summary of cultural factors which support and which negate family planning see Miriam T. Manisoff, ed., *Family Planning Training for Social Service: A Teaching Guide in Family Planning* (New York: Planned Parenthood—World Population, 1970).

[22] Soemardjan, *op. cit.*

apply to their countries. This does not deny the importance of the cultural variables, but reaffirms the need to understand them within the context of a particular society or group of people. There were a few participants who did not share the general enthusiasm for the Conference objectives, particularly those concerned with attitudinal changes of populations in respect to population control. The objectives in question were those which assumed that population should be controlled and that social work was somehow to be involved in bringing about attitudinal shifts that would cause greater voluntary change in conception patterns. The dissenters questioned whether attitudinal changes were as important as all that and stressed that whenever family planning methods had become widely available families tended to make fairly prompt use of them to the end that they had smaller families. But these comments ran against the current of most experience described by those deeply involved in actual family planning programs.

Role of Social Workers in Formulating Policies and Programs

The contribution of social workers to population policies and family planning programs can be made at two quite different levels, according to Aida Gindy.[23] The first, or "macro" level, involves few people but takes up the highly critical task of determining policies and devising programs of both the national governmental type and the private voluntary type. The second, or "micro" level, deals with implementation of programs by large numbers of practitioners through counseling, changing community attitudes toward large families, and breaking down other barriers to acceptance of family-limiting services.

Given the characteristics of population activities and family planning programs and the cultural and psychological variables assisting or impeding their effectiveness, what can social workers offer as part of an interdisciplinary team? The answer includes the attitudes and values which social workers bring to such an assignment as they are just as real as the attitudes of officials and the general public previously discussed. Conference documents abound with references to this matter. Herman Stein, speaking as the Conference rapporteur, referred to some social work values that had been highlighted in the discussions:

> Family well-being and family welfare are higher values than population policy for social workers.
>
> Freedom and self-determination are important values. The former

[23] Aida Gindy, "Social Work Roles and Opportunities for Service," *supra*, pp. 82-91.

rests on knowledge and the possibility of options. Ignorance is not a freedom. Self-determination includes, among other things, the right of communities to participate in a judgment on the policies which affect them.

Social workers prefer voluntarism and choice.

The social work profession is moving toward a greater stress on the preventive and developmental functions of social work.

Social workers recognize the necessity for working with and learning from other disciplines and professions, without too much concern about which profession is more important or central.

Social workers recognize the unique value of paraprofessional case aides, volunteers, and all others not professionally trained who can be encompassed within the social welfare manpower to make a contribution to family planning.

Edwin F. Daily of the New York City Department of Health, in a preliminary statement prepared for the Conference, obtained the views of a social work colleague, Frances Dresher, on the social work contribution to family planning service. She listed the following:

1. Knowledge of social, emotional, and cultural characteristics of individuals and population as influencing social functioning—specifically translated into the human and social requirements of daily living.
2. A systematic and practical approach to problem-solving that works equally well in identifying anticipated problems in programs and services.
3. A knowledge and art in communication with individuals and groups that permits a more effective transmission of information and the reduction of resistances to utilizing services.
4. An ability to serve as coordinator, mediator, enabler, advocate, administrator, educator, and in several other roles for which the situation may call.

Over and over again social work participants stated how much they could help at the macro level, where their services were little used. They admitted that at the micro, or practitioner level, they needed to improve competence in the specifics of family planning. In a strange fashion schools of social work have shied away from all references to sexuality and its centrality to the human condition. This situation needs correction if family planning is to be viewed as part of family welfare.[24]

One of the four discussion groups of the Conference dealt with "The Social Worker in Social Policy and Social Planning." In its final report it

---

[24] Lydia Rapoport, "Education and Training of Social Workers For Roles and Functions in Family Planning," *supra,* pp. 124-141.

distinguishes between social policy and social planning:

> **Social Policy:** The complex of public social goals and priorities and their supporting instruments.
>
> **Social Planning:** The deliberate conscious series of processes undertaken to formulate order and to organize a social policy design, either public or voluntary.

Its major recommendations fit well into a series of suggested roles derived from an analysis of other Conference documents. These recommendations are: identification of social policy issues and statement of goals; selecting and assigning auspices or sponsors for the programs; developing a strategy for change called for by the program; planning for the staff and its training; conducting research and evaluation to ensure more effective planning; working out plans for liaison and communication.

Identification of Social Policy Issues And Statement of Goals

Vera Shlakman has pointed out the overlapping and sometimes apparently contradictory purposes advocated in the family planning literature: "Family planning policy is being urged (1) to assure that every child is 'wanted'; (2) to free women from the drudgery of chronic pregnancy and the requirement of bearing a child against their wills; (3) to reduce child dependency, that is, to cut public welfare costs; (4) to reduce the social costs of child rearing; (5) to reduce poverty; (6) to prevent illegitimacy; (7) to foster the health and happiness of families by spacing pregnancies; (8) to encourage families not to have more children than they can afford; (9) to enhance family well-being by reducing the size of families; (10) to protect maternal health; (11) to prevent defects through reduction of births to every young or older mothers, and to others who are at risk, and through gentic counseling; (12) to offer to every couple the opportunity to realize the size of family to which it aspires; and (13) to control total population."[25]

In the sorting out of priorities—a necessary step in designing an effective program—social workers can help other disciplines keep in their purview the human element which might otherwise be overshadowed by the magnitude and urgency of the problems of population control. One participant observed: "It is the appreciation of the human needs and feelings of the couples involved and an understanding of the psychological, social, and cultural values which influence their attitudes and behavior

---

[25] Vera Shlakman, "Social Work's Role in Family Planning: Social Policy Issues," in Haselkorn, *op. cit.*, p. 71.

that will affect the ultimate success of any family planning program." Another participant thought that social workers can and do resist certain temptations that allegedly may persuade some to think of the pill as a substitute for the provision of decent social services (or income) or to think simplistically that all of our social and environmental problems will submit to the panacea of a reduced birth rate. Furthermore, social workers who have responsibility for helping to design policies and programs in any field of welfare must be aware of the population and/or fertility effects of programs directed to other social objectives (e.g., income) and to facilitate the inclusion of desirable population sub-objectives in these programs. Social workers can also take more initiative in building family planning service into the delivery of other services such as day care programs or any new family assistance plans that may be developed in the United States.

In the statement of goals for family planning programs, social workers can also be sure that all segments of the population have access to the benefits provided, that delivery systems are adequate, and that the programs do not lower birth rates of any group in a discriminatory fashion.

Determining Program Sponsorship or Auspices

The auspices may be public or private, or the program may involve a mixture of both. If voluntary, it may single out one organization or seek a combination of several organizations willing to cooperate. The program may be centered in the health subsystem or the welfare subsystem of the society, or it may appropriately bridge the two. In each country some agencies seem to do a better job with population or family planning programs than do others. For example, one state welfare director speaking at an earlier conference took the position that, in the United States: "Auspice is a determining factor. Where public welfare or public health programs are locally administered, positive policies of a state department may not be enthusiastically implemented, if at all. But under a state administration with a positive policy, chances for implementation on a broad base are more likely."[26]

If the development of programs for family planning is basically the same as program planning for other health and welfare services, as some writers claim,[27] then social workers bring a rich experience to bear on the

---

[26] Norman V. Lourie, "The Responsibility of Public Welfare in Family Planning," in Haselkorn, *op. cit.*, p. 103.

[27] Helen P. Stanford, "Program Planning for Family Planning," in Varela, *op. cit.*, p. 9.

decision-making about the selection of sponsoring ministries, agencies, or private associations, as well as the best ways of assuring coordination among all of those groups participating in the program.

Needless to say, the more important family planning programs become in a given country, the greater the number of public and private agencies wanting to have a part in them. Social workers can help assess the contribution that each agency can make in terms of its previous experience and competence and see that the program which is planned is so fashioned that it makes use of the strengths of all of these groups. In this phase of planning, it is more useful to combine skill in community organization with specialized clinical skills of the medical profession.

Developing a Strategy for Change

Population policies and family planning programs seek to persuade people to adopt effective birth control techniques which they have not used before, to change their value system to the point that they will accept smaller and better-spaced families, and to place the welfare of the whole family above immediate personal gratification. To reach larger numbers of people, organizations which have developed delivery techniques for a particular group may have to modify those techniques quite drastically. In fact, the strategy which social workers can help devise is that of confronting the cultural obstacles already described in considerable detail. Herman Stein reminds us that, in any social change, resistance is inevitable. "If anything is important in the way of planned change it will evoke resistance. If there is no opposition, the chances are that one is not dealing with anything so terribly significant."[28] The import of this observation is that social workers assisting in program planning must more and more accept the fact of conflict and even work with a conflict model of change.

A strategy of change also involves realistic assessment of power and how it is to be brought into play once a program gets underway. The political power of the state is one example. The power of the religious organization to paralyze the power of the state as far as family planning is concerned must be recognized in some countries. The power of other interests will vary markedly from country to country, but should not be overlooked. This calls for social workers to assume much more of an analytic role than they have in the past. Such a role was advocated strongly by the discussion group on social policy and social planning, which also suggested that social workers work responsibly, sensitively,

---

[28] Stein, *op. cit.*

and knowledgeably with the power structure in order to gain support for social development goals.

The same group recommended that, as the strategy is being developed, social workers serve in the advocacy role in behalf of the population policies that reflect the values of the profession. In Pakistan, it seems that there is a definite swing toward the client-centered approach in place of the clinic-centered approach. This means that the stress is more upon the feelings, needs, and desires of the people than upon arguments in behalf of the superiority of particular contraceptive techniques which may be adopted through a mass advertising campaign. What is needed, the Pakistani participants declared, is the personal touch which social workers traditionally provide, one which fits family planning into the total life context of the family to be helped.

A test of any strategy for change, embodied in a visible program, is the number of dropouts among those whom the program is supposed to serve. Social workers might well try to discover whether new approaches would lead to fewer failures in the program. Here one is dealing with human motivation, which is complex at best, but of much concern to change agents whether they be social workers or any other professional group.

Another facet of power is coercion. Some population experts, such as Kingsley Davis, argue that voluntary family planning programs are not sufficient in scope or effective enough to meet the population crisis. He believes coercive measures must be taken to force people to behave in such a way that fertility will be controlled. Social workers need, of course, to examine such positions even though they run counter to their basic humanistic approach. In some of them may be found program ideas which need to be adopted, though preserving as much individual freedom as possible.

Staffing the Program and Developing Training Procedures for Staff

The planning team will of course determine what staff is needed to do the jobs that are drawn up in keeping with financial and other resources provided. The social work role is to see that certain types of personnel are included—personnel who see the human and not merely the demographic or technical dimensions of the problem. One cannot prescribe in advance just what the manpower requirements of any program will be, but one can speak with considerable assurance about the training needed. A key word in this connection is *orientation.* One participant from India suggested three types: (1) orientation of community leaders and non-officials through seminars and workshops in order to promote understanding of the program and to gain their cooperation; (2) orientation of the program personnel in social work methods so that they may have an adequate understanding of them and their possible contribution to the program; and (3) orientation of teachers of schools of social work in the various aspects of the health and family planning program.

Almost every commentator on social work roles stressed the training contribution. For several countries, detailed training plans were presented in the Conference documentation. Some of these will be taken up in a later section on social work roles in the implementation of the program. However, a part of the planning function certainly is to work out the procedures by which the program staff is trained for its responsibilities, is sensitized to the many social variables which impinge upon the operation of the program, and is given an awareness of its own importance in making the program a success.

Miss Gindy, in her Conference paper, devotes much attention to the various levels of social work training and the contribution that those from different levels can make to population policy and to family planning programs. She deals, also, with paraprofessionals and with volunteers. Social workers with experience in complex welfare programs should be able to designate how staff members of various education and kinds of competence can fit into the overall program design. Demographers, planning economists, lawyers who draft legislation, and officials charged for the first time with the administration of such programs are not apt to understand the significance or even the interrelationships among staff members at different levels of responsibility, but without the paraprofessional and volunteer, the outreach of most programs is not very wide.[29]

Research and Evaluation Roles

Research is beginning to have the same attraction in social work as it has in many other fields. It is one channel through which a person can move out of the practitioner role; other channels are administration or advanced higher education. So it is not surprising to find social workers from many countries urging that their skill in research and evaluation be recognized and utilized. And in several cases it has been, as some highly competent studies show.

Whether a social worker perceives himself as a researcher or not, he

[29] For an exciting program using the community aide on a paid basis, see Edwin F. Daily and Aileen Sirey, *A Description of the First City-wide Program for the Initiation of Contraception Before Hopital Discharge* (New York: Maternity and Infant Care Family Planning Projects, City of New York Dept. of Health, 1970). Mimeographed.

certainly should be aware of the need for data on which sound planning must be based. The social worker can ask the hard question: Why did you choose this alternative instead of that? Where is the information to support such a decision? Also, a social worker should be able to look at two different studies, both of which may come out with different conclusions, and determine which is more apt to describe social reality and be a fitting guide for planning. Another failure which needs correction is the insufficient investment in analyzing the range of results that are likely to come from technological change. A narrowly structured family planning program might succeed in a technical sense but the social effects of its innovations may be more pronounced or of a different kind than anticipated.

Evaluation, a special kind of research, needs to be built into program operation from the beginning. Results as determined at different stages of the project should be assessed and the program modified if necessary. Social workers, rather than resenting efforts at evaluation, can play a useful role in insisting that it be included at the outset; they can periodically interpret the results to be sure that the goals which they consider important are being achieved.

Miss Gindy has indicated how social workers can contribute their expertise to the comprehensive research which determines national population policies and plans. She mentions in particular studies on attitudinal change, family size and patterns, size and structures of families and households, and the relation of different types of family unions to fertility levels, husband-wife relationships, and attitudes to children. Other areas which she mentions include those affecting the youth population, for example, attitudes toward sex, unmarried mothers, and needs associated with the growing numbers of young people—employment, education, social aspirations, and views on justice. Research also needs to be done on new functions and roles of family and child welfare services in the implementation of family planning programs. To sociologists, anthropologists, psychologists, and others who might tell social workers that they are already taking care of this research, Miss Gindy would say that the social worker is well-equipped to participate because the profession has built up a unique knowledge of the individual, his human behavior, feelings, values, attitudes, anxieties, and marital relationships. She has staked the claim; let the discussion rage.

Liaison and Communication Roles

Social workers with experience in community development programs can testify to the risk that program planners run when they do not take the wishes and fears of the program clientele into account. Simply deciding for people is not taking them into account, but involving them in many aspects of the planning, where this can be done, does test out various program ideas. Social workers see themselves as playing this communication role primarily because they have an understanding of the people whom the program is supposed to serve, whereas officials and national planners may be much too far removed to understand the actual conditions of everyday life. The translation of a program from its beautifully bound statement into human behavior is usually left to various practitioners, who—curiously enough—may never be asked to participate in the planning at all. Thus, a program can be seen as a constantly changing approach to a social problem, with much continuity to be sure, but some modification as feedback flows from the participants to the decision-makers and as the problems faced by the decision-makers (shortage of funds, personnel, etc.) get interpreted to the participants. This leads, of course, to the practitioner role to be discussed in a later section.

The social worker also thinks of himself as well-equipped to be a liaison person among many professional groups, each with its own perspective which must be taken into account by others. A program which depends upon government, medicine, law, and social work—to mention but four facets—is an exercise in interprofessional dialogue to which we next turn.

THE IMPLEMENTING ROLE OF SOCIAL WORK

Although the role of social work has been minimal in policy planning and program development, it has assumed some importance in several countries at the operating practitioner level. It is in such a setting that the social worker is often a member of an interprofessional team since most programs involve personnel from the fields of medicine, public health, and education, as well as welfare. Therefore, before looking at the special social work roles in program implementation, one might see the interprofessional relationships or network in which these are carried out.

The Interprofessional Dialogue

Much stress has already been placed in this report on the international, cross-cultural nature of the Conference. Many references have been made to aspects of population policy and family planning programs pointed out by representatives of many countries, but not much has been said thus far about the interdisciplinary, interprofessional character of the Conference, which was one of its most significant features. Those attending knew from the pre-Conference material that the focus was to be on social work, particularly what schools of social work in the United States could learn from people at home and abroad about ways of preparing social workers more effectively for service in population and family planning programs. At first, the physicians, social scientists, nurses, and other non-social workers thought that their chief function would be to provide background material to the Conference, but as they became caught up in the Conference activities they realized that the social workers really wanted these guests from many countries to help them do a serious task of soul-searching, of discovering their own identity as it related to population dynamics, and of suggesting how they might participate usefully in existing programs as well as in those yet to be designed. Such considerations, it was understood, would be translated into recommendations for schools of social work in the United States, which admittedly had done almost nothing to prepare social workers for such programs.

One part of the Conference was purposely devoted to an interprofessional panel whose members were given the opportunity of stressing what their own professions were doing and how social work could emulate or develop its own distinctive contributions. Like many panels, the main purpose was not achieved, although many interesting subsidiary results did add materially to the subsequent discussion. One problem was that some panel members also found it necessary to be spokesmen for their countries, so that their remarks about various programs could be put into proper perspective. Some shared with the Conference their own rich experience in the family planning field. Without trying to cover all of the ideas presented by panel members, we can at least reflect some of their concerns.

Laila S. El Hamamsy, an anthropologist from the United Arab Republic, was interested in research projects which would provide the data on which good programs must be based; she was also disturbed by some of the inept methods which family planning personnel used in communicating with their clients because they had not thought about the existing culture patterns. She suggested that social workers might be doing more research on such areas as family structure, the role of women, and the real meaning of children as they affected woman's status.

Harriet Pilpel, a lawyer from the United States who has worked during the past thirty years as legal counsel for local, national, and international planned parenthood bodies, impressed the Conference deeply by the way she traced shifting public acceptance of family planning. At first, she pointed out, the keynote was prohibition. You shall not practice birth control, you shall not have abortions. The prohibition was based on the tenet that it was sinful to engage in sex for recreation and not procreation purposes. From prohibition we moved to a kind of privileged status for birth control in the United States, shifting the emphasis from morality or immorality to what was medically indicated. The doctors could decide who was entitled to birth control. Today we have reached the third stage, which defines birth control as a matter of human right. Mrs. Pilpel expressed a temptation to editorialize in this connection. With this third stage, social workers feel very comfortable, but if there is a fourth stage on the horizon—the obligation to practice birth control in keeping with new strong social sanctions—the social work profession would have to undergo a shift in value orientation. This raises the very difficult question: What is the social worker's chief concern? Is it the rights of the particular individual client or the rights of society at large?

The legal profession, like social work, in Mrs. Pilpel's view, has been conspicuous for its lack of involvement in family planning to date. But this does not mean that law is an unimportant part of the interprofessional dialogue. Most legislators in the United States are lawyers. All judges are lawyers. Most men at the top level of administration and executive positions, such as the President of the United States, are lawyers. Laws have a significant influence on behavior and therefore are important in the whole field which we are discussing.

Eugen Pusic, a professor of public administration from Yugoslavia, told of the problems facing administrators in his country when confronting population questions there. First, there was a wide diversity in rates of growth, from 1.1 percent in one part of the country to 2.8 percent elsewhere. What are the objective conditions which determine the attitudes of people toward children, family size, and the like? Should administrators take it upon themselves to try to change these conditions, these attitudes? These are difficult questions to answer, and they illustrate philosophical and practical considerations which invariably enter into administrative decisions.

A social welfare worker from Uganda, Eric P. Kibuka, cited the current population growth rate of 3 percent per annum. This growth rate reflects in part the constant migration of people from the neighboring countries, but it would also appear to reflect the values and attitudes people hold in respect to family size. However, with changing conditions, new values and new problems arise. Thus, for instance, according to the customs of the various African societies and/or communities of Uganda, all children are born legitimate and are accepted and claimed by their respective fathers—the concept of illegitimacy is almost unknown. Now, however, some unmarried mothers cannot identify the fathers of their children, nor do some men accept paternity of children born out of wedlock. This panelist's comments vividly illustrated the linkage between public welfare issues and population issues. As much as anyone at the Conference, he saw limits to voluntarism and suggested some coercion in order to achieve a common good. The rights of the community (social obligations), he argued, should not be countermanded by individual rights.

Joseph Beasley, a physician from the United States, stressed the importance of developing the potential of people who are yet to be born and a concern for the human beings already here. He thought that the United States faced a major population problem and explained that he was devoting his energies to at least four programs, each of which dealt with some aspects of population policy. He indicated that in the 1930s medicine had a great concern for infertility, but the emphasis has now shifted, with much more attention being given to sterilization as one of the safest and best methods of family planning after people have completed their desired childbearing period. In his program he is trying to de-physicianize the process. It is better to have a trained person spend an hour with a patient explaining matters than to have a harried physician pat her on the head, say that she will be all right, and then disappear into the next room. He viewed overpopulation as a condition in which a country was not fully developing the potential of each child, for whom the cost of investment is going up every year.

The panel moderator, Bess Dana, a social worker with experience in interdisciplinary education and practice, reminded the Conference that irritations, frustrations, perplexities, and complexities sometimes overwhelm us. We need to think about making the interprofessional dialogue a part of education itself. The process must be initiated early so that interdisciplinary cooperation becomes part of professional preparation. There is waste in duplication of effort now existing in professional schools, and there is also omission of much content that should be offered.

At the end of the panel discussion, Ruby Pernell, the chairman of the general session, observed that no member of the panel had told social workers what they ought to be doing; that this kind of interdisciplinary dialogue should be transferred from Conferences such as this to university campuses. The original purpose of the university was to bring together a group of scholars addressed to the purpose of common social purposes. Certainly population policy deserves the attention of the university community to a degree not hitherto in evidence.

The interprofessional panel was, of course, presenting viewpoints to the whole Conference. It was when the participants began to interact as members of the four discussion groups that they focused much more attention on social work contributions. The discussion group on social work service to individuals, families, groups, and communities reflected the effort to identify the social work evolution in direct service. Its report stated that the task is complicated by the interdisciplinary nature of the problem and expanding use of subprofessionals. There was no question, however, about the fact that social work can bring its understanding of and distinct focus on the psychosocial aspects of reproductive behavior and family life, its value and ethical base, and its skills in working with individuals and families, groups and communities. In response to the concern among some family planning advocates that social work may tend toward an overemphasis on motivational factors and counseling approaches, the group emphasized that guarding individualization in the delivery of service should not be equated with direct face-to-face service with all who need and want family planning service.

The discussion group on manpower planning tried to identify a special role for social work. It agreed on a gamut of manpower tasks that could be filled by social workers but questioned whether they could claim that only social work personnel had the necessary training and skills with reference to specific family planning tasks. The contributions of social work are a matter of degree rather than exclusive preparation for functioning in this developing field.

The discussion group on social policy and social planning was concerned about the knowledge and research experience of social workers. They found it embarrassing to realize how dependent they were on their United Nations specialist and a physician who had given long leadership in the family planning movement. Some even felt that they were learning the rudiments of population policy and family planning from these experts during the discussion sessions.

Miss Gindy's Conference paper also addressed itself to social welfare personnel as members of interdisciplinary teams. With their involvement in the broad objectives of national development, they face the challenge of working in closer coordination with allied professions. She indicated that interdisciplinary relationships take various forms. First, there is the cooperative relationship among different professionals engaged in implementing sectoral objectives. An effort is made here to avoid duplication, conflict, or absence of services on the part of the different sectors. Second, there is the relationship in which each discipline works to integrate parts of a whole program meaningfully so that one measure reinforces or complements another. Thus, a welfare worker may learn how to teach better health habits or a health worker may know how to promote better social relationships within the family. The two workers learn to make their knowledge areas and skills complementary in reinforcing overall objectives. In many large-scale programs the interdisciplinary approach becomes incorporated in the intermediate worker whose training combines content from two or three fields.

From time to time, particularly in informal conversations, participants mentioned the difficulties social workers faced in population or family planning programs which were dominated by the medical or public health professions. In fact, some gave this as an important reason why social work had not become more involved in such programs. Social workers want to be accepted as professionals in their own right. Yet, Herman Stein suggested in his Conference summary that social workers should not be too worried if they were considered ancillary personnel in such programs. After all, to be ancillary means to be helpful and that is what social workers hope to be. The non-social workers remarked on the degree to which their social work conferees avoided the charge of waving their professional banner, of asserting their proprietary rights. Instead, in matters bearing on population policy and in family planning services, they were genuinely interested in being members of an interdisciplinary team.

In the professional dialogue, participants not in social work were generous in their comments on the social work role. A practicing lawyer wrote:

> 1. The social worker is an absolutely necessary intermediary between the professions and the users of professional services. Doctors, lawyers, and others are not known for their ability to communicate to persons outside their own professions, and in this area of interpretation and communication back and forth, it seems to me that the social worker is indispensable.
>
> 2. Second, it also seems to me that the social worker knows better than any other person the attitudinal and other blocks which may stand in the way of the acceptance and use of population and family planning services. In other words, in addition to being the purveyor of information back and forth between other professions and the service users, the social worker is in the best position to ascertain what services are needed and how they can be most effectively delivered.
>
> 3. It would seem to me that greater liaison between the social work profession and the other groups involved in population and family planning is badly needed. A special group has been set up allying lawyers and social workers in the field of matrimonial law. It would seem to me that a more inclusive liaison of doctors, demographers, lawyers, social workers, and social scientists is a goal which should be implemented as soon as possible.

An educator wrote:

> What we have seen in the United States is the development of services, increased acceptance, public education, training, etc. for family planning through the acceptance of responsibility for these areas mainly by the health disciplines—medicine, nursing, health education, public health administration. Unless social work and related education defines its own role and acceptance of responsi-

bility for some of the areas which need its competence and moves rapidly toward implementing this responsibility, then family planning and population may well proceed without it. But an opportunity will have been lost.

A public health nurse in commenting on the Conference theme wrote:

> Generally, social workers in departments of public welfare have worked cooperatively with departments of health in the development of joint family planning programs. This has been true on the national level and in some local areas. At the local level, there seems to be mutual agreement regarding the urgent need for these services; but frequently, the pace of in-service preparation of professional workers has not been coordinated with the implementation of the programs.
>
> I believe there needs to be increased activity on the part of social workers in promoting family planning education and services. . . . Awareness on their part of the meaning of a new child to any family with whom they are counselling will broaden their contribution to that family, allowing their care to be more complete.
>
> As a public health nurse I see the goals of our two professions as very similar—to prevent the breakdown of physical and social factors which impede the growth of individuals, families, and communities, and also to improve the quality of life. Surely there are needs for better understanding of the contributions of each profession and needs for learning new ways to coordinate our activities. Activities in family planning might well serve as a major coordinating impetus.

So the dialogue continued: in the corridors of the East-West Center, over coffee, or in leisurely conversations on the hotel terrace. In fact, many of the most important explorations of interprofessional roles were unofficial and not a part of the Conference documentation.

The Implementing Roles of Social Work

In many preceding sections, almost to the point of redundancy, we have stressed the social work perspective, experience, and training which can be applied to population questions and family planning programs at the macro level. Here the emphasis is upon operational roles, which may parallel the policy or planning roles, but at a much more concrete or micro level. Miss Gindy, in her Conference paper, said that the direct contribution the social worker can make to family planning is centered primarily on his attributes and skills as a practitioner. By virtue of their profession, social welfare personnel are human relations specialists and are involved in the daily lives of individuals, families, and communities at large.

Such competence is taken into account in the brief characterization of the practitioner roles discussed at the Conference. In reviewing the list two things are obvious: first, almost any social worker could have drawn up a similar list, for it contains the commonplace contributions of the profession; second, few of these roles are the exclusive prerogative of social work but are definitely within its purview. The order of presentation has no significance.

1. *Counseling of individuals and families who have problems in relation to family planning.* This can be done through regular welfare programs where family planning is one facet of the total situation in which the client finds himself, or the counseling can be a built-in feature of the family planning program itself. In the former case, the social worker may refer the client to a family planning program for particular assistance. At times this referral has been a bit confusing. Bernard Greenblatt writes:

> The major argument against caseworker initiative is that providing information or referral may encroach upon the moral or religious belief of the client. A more "practical" consideration is that if a client is referred against her inclination, she may not be strongly motivated to accept and retain the contraceptive device or advice.
>
> Proponents of worker initiative argue that clients not requesting information are not disinclined, but do not know what to ask about. A basic reason for worker initiative is that contraceptive information should be provided when 'professionally indicated.' The client's right to know—in order to achieve the secular objective 'freedom' to choose the number and spacing of . . . children—harmonizes completely, the proponents assume, with the obligation not to withhold professional information.[30]

Katherine B. Oettinger sees the counseling function as making use of family planning to augment the social work aim of rehabilitating the family disrupted by social and emotional stress. She states:

> The mission of family planning impinges directly on the mission of preventive social work: to bypass a measure of personal and community ills by eradicating some of the root causes of social pathology.
>
> And when it falls to the lot of the social worker to help families stabilize lives already disrupted by social and emotional stress, family planning can also be a means to augment the social work aim of rehabilitating the family.
>
> Certainly, by offering means for control of fertility and, with it, some ordering of destiny, a third social work goal is achieved: equal opportunity for all sectors of the population. Helping those buffeted by fate to overcome their sense of helplessness has new meaning now that technological advances permit a growing variety of safe

---

[30] Bernard Greenblatt, "Policy Issues in Welfare Referrals to Birth Control Programs," *The Catholic Charities Review* (January, 1969), n.p. Also see Gitta Meier, "Implementing the Objectives of Family Planning Programs," *Social Casework* (April, 1969), pp. 195-203.

> and effective methods acceptable for meeting individual differences. To do this, basic social work education must race to keep pace with modern scientific findings, with changes in ideology, and with growing federal support in delivery of family planning services.[31]

Counseling, moreover, can prove an integral part of a family planning program itself. Experience in Hong Kong and Pakistan, to mention but two programs, indicates that the more time-consuming counseling (in comparison with brief contacts) achieves higher long-term results. More women use the services offered and do not drop out of the program. Public health people, aware of the tremendous job to be done, argue that the client counseling service cannot be the only approach because it is expensive, not enough professional caseworkers are available, and too few people can be reached quickly. Yet, it is more and more being accepted as a legitimate feature of family planning programs. Social work schools, therefore, must prepare more graduates who can function in the family planning centers, in health centers, post-partum hospital clinics, and other places where the message and services of clinicians can be communicated.[32]

2. *Community support, client contact, and motivation.* Although in part this overlaps the counseling role, it goes far beyond it. In this role the social worker helps develop educational techniques and works with local leaders (village headmen, county officials, presidents of voluntary organizations, etc.) through the application of community development techniques. The aim is to develop the climate of opinion which legitimates and provides acceptance of population policies or a family planning program. In this connection extensive reference could be made to community development literature prepared by social workers, but few citations now refer specifically to family planning programs. Much more thought needs to be given in most countries to this practitioner role.

3. *Documentation of program activities, client responses, and organizational obstacles encountered.* Without such documentation, evaluation and some types of research are not possible. In such a role, social workers are able to provide feedback and suggested changes to those guiding the programs and dispensing various kinds of services. Related to this is the preparation by social workers of proposals for experimentation with different approaches and their evaluation.

4. *Administering population and family planning programs at the local,*

---

[31] Katherine Brownell Oettinger, "The School of Social Work Responsibilities in Family Planning Education" (Washington, D.C.: U.S. Department of Health, Education and Welfare, 1968), p. 3.

[32] See Manisoff, *Family Planning . . ., op. cit.,* Chapter V, "Suggestions for Working with Clients," pp. 49-61.

district, or county level. By their training and experience, many social workers are equipped to serve in administrative capacities. They can be as effective program directors as those trained in medicine, education, or some other professional field. In such a capacity they need to work with a multi-professional staff and deal with extra-program problems (political process, public relations, etc.) as well as with the internal operation of the program.

5. *Training of existing staff (in-service) and of trainees.* The social work practitioner can impart particularly the non-clinical, social aspects of the program. He is also able to put the technical details into a much broader family life education context. From many countries at the Conference came testimony of the utility to the programs of the social work training role. Here, too, the distinctions between the professionally trained social worker, the paraprofessional worker, and the volunteer need to be made. In fact, there is some evidence that the greatest impact a relatively few social workers can have on a program is not to try themselves to be the functionaries who contact clients and follow up their clinical visits, but rather to train the paraprofessionals who are much closer in life style and background to the clients.

6. *Supervision of field work trainees and paraprofessional staff.* Although this could be considered part of training, some programs call for field work supervision of staff already employed and trained. Participants at the Hawaii Conference mentioned several times the need to use men as part of the field work staff since they are able to make contacts which the women social workers are unable to make.

7. *Coordination of the population program and family planning services with programs of other agencies and developing better understanding of fertility control among all concerned.* The assumption is often implicitly made that the people who need education about the importance of family planning and other population measures are the possible adopters of contraceptive techniques. Often, workers who touch the lives of families through other fields need basic information, too. Cooperative relationships among appropriate agencies can be arranged only if their perceptions are clear. Social workers are skilled at this task.

There are many other duties which could be dignified as specific social work roles, but the ones mentioned above provide the spectrum of contribution at the operating level. No social worker is himself equipped to do all of these tasks equally well, for social work is represented in a range of specialized activities. However, some social workers have the experience to play any of the roles mentioned.

In the soul-searching that went on in the discussion groups, Conference participants told themselves—and quite correctly, too—that in playing these practitioner roles they hoped not merely to perform the technical part of the role adequately, but, in doing so, to convey a sense of human warmth and to build up the dignity of those with whom they dealt. This capacity extends to relations with colleagues from various professions as well as to clients. And when individuals were pressed to explain why they thought that they could do so well, they invariably attributed it to the kind of education they had had in schools of social work. As far as specific family planning preparation is concerned, however, some of the glow disappears since schools of social work have, for the most part, done little or nothing along this line. What should they do? The Hawaii Conference did come up with a few answers.

WHAT SCHOOLS OF SOCIAL WORK SHOULD BE DOING

A Preliminary Survey

In preparation for the Conference, the Council on Social Work Education made an informal survey of what schools of social work in the United States were doing to prepare their students for work on population problems in family planning programs.[33] Out of eighty schools contacted, twenty responded, but these included most of those visibly involved in such preparation. After analyzing the data Lydia Rapoport came to these conclusions:

> 1. The amount of activity in curriculum development and teaching in family planning and population dynamics depends heavily at this point in time on the availability of faculty leadership, competence, and commitment. Usually, there is one key person who gives impetus and direction. With the loss of the key person the whole program or emphasis is lost.
>
> 2. There is probably more being done on population and family planning, on a low visibility level, than has been reported. At present, the prevailing pattern is of integration and diffusion of content throughout the sequences along which social work education is currently structured. The question arises as to whether a school can do justice to a newly emerging area of practice and social concern, unless, at least for developmental purposes, it is packaged as a specialty area for purposes of development of relevant knowledge and refinement of content and method. The trend in social work education has been for the past several decades toward the absorption of the specialty content into an integrated curriculum after sizeable experience with it.

---

[33] The Conference paper by Lydia Rapoport, "Education and Training of Social Workers for Roles and Functions in Family Planning," should be read in its entirety as a background to this section. *Supra*, pp. 124-141.

3. At present, there seems to be more visible interest and activity in a school of social work in regard to family planning and population dynamics when the school is located in proximity to a school of public health or a center of population research. The reasons are obvious in regard to availability of expertness and manpower resources and stimulation through ongoing research and practice.

4. Many schools referred to individual student interest in this subject which is often met through individualized assignments in class. It would seem that such student interest could be stimulated and strengthened. This would be especially feasible as schools move into the direction of greater flexibility in curriculum structuring. This growing trend should get further impetus from the Council on Social Work Education's new Statement on Curriculum Policy, 1970.

5. Faculty can only give leadership to the necessary developmental tasks as they consciously prepare themselves through mechanisms of research, community consultation, continuing and advanced education and teaching roles, through continuing education under various sponsorships as a trial run for content, bibliographic materials, and possible new teaching roles via new approaches.

6. If the profession of social work is to play a significant role in family planning and in problems of social policy in population problems, the graduate schools of social work will have to make a sustained effort far beyond what is being done now, according to the trends in this survey. The efforts at present are still rather hit and miss, or occasional and opportunistic in nature. There needs to be more basic education for everyone in this area, plus an opportunity of choice for students to develop specialist knowledge and competence.

Discussion Group Recommendations

These conclusions provided the springboard for lengthy and stimulating discussion in the four discussion groups about specific recommendations on social work education. Their findings can best be treated in terms of the issues raised instead of by presenting all of the details which some of the groups produced. After all, as Arnulf M. Pins, chairman of the group on administration and program planning, observed: "We cannot revise the social work curriculum for individual schools at this Conference." Once this was accepted, the conferees were ready to deal with issues instead of trying to prepare curricular blueprints. The Conference as a whole did not attempt to agree upon any set of recommendations but left it up to each group to do this in the light of the particular theme assigned to it. Some issues which emerged were:

1. *Content or subject-matter on population dynamics and family planning to be covered by the student.* One discussion group reported that all social workers should have knowledge and understanding of

population dynamics and the major cause and consequences of problems in this area which may exist in their country, their geographic region, or the world as a whole. Social workers should also have knowledge and understanding of why family planning is important to persons, to families, and to countries from a health, economic, and social viewpoint and some understanding of this relationship to social work. In addition, they should know about and understand the values and cultural factors and issues which affect this area, as well as the different services and programs that exist.

There was much discussion in some groups as to how far schools of social work should go in dealing with human sexuality and contraceptive techniques. Several participants raised the question as to why social work schools seem to skirt sex when it is central to many family problems with which their clients are trying to cope. As for contraception, it was agreed that any course content along this line should be taught by people who were technically competent. But a caveat was registered as to the danger of teaching only very specific techniques, many of which may be outdated in a very few years.

One group concurred in the urgency of providing students with conceptual analytic and research tools to assist social workers in moving from the case approach and from the stance of emotional speculation to systematic study of outcome and consequences.

2. *Strategy for including content in the curriculum.* The possibilities suggested were developing new courses, adding content to existing courses, or simply new perspectives in handling existing content. One group recommended that some family planning and population dynamics content should be integrated into all relevant aspects of the curriculum for social work students. In addition, certain content areas, such as demography, which cuts across all practice areas, may be offered as a separate course in a school of social work, or made available through other school or university departments. Specialized courses in family planning and population dynamics may be offered for students who would like to pursue this area further or specialize in it and for students seeking advanced study in this area. It was also urged that interdisciplinary learning experiences be provided both in class and field.

3. *Relating population dynamics and family planning content to existing subject matter taught.* One way to state this issue is not to ask how can the curriculum be modified in order to include material on population dynamics and family planning, but rather how can this material be used to enrich, round out, and make more relevant the subject matter already being covered. Certainly, the population problem will become even more acute and professionals from many fields will be increasingly concerned

with aspects of it. If the standard courses do not recognize this problem, then they are deficient to that extent.

Connected with this, of course, is the observation that much of the knowledge and skill required to deal with social aspects of family planning programs are not solely identified with such programs but are part of the general social work background with applicability to several fields. It is important, according to some of the Conference participants, for illustrations and cases showing such applicability to be drawn from the areas of population dynamics and family planning.

There were many other issues which were mentioned but not treated extensively: the degree to which schools of social work, or at least a few of them interested in this specialty, might prepare students directly for careers in population dynamics and family planning; the importance of field instruction as a means of acquainting all students with population phenomena and family planning services; the preparation of teaching materials, which are in short supply as far as social work approaches to population and family planning are concerned; in-service and continuing education; and the leadership schools of social work should take in seeing that the field of social work as a whole is better equipped to cooperate in population programs and family planning services.

Behind these suggestions to schools of social work is a sense of urgency. It was agreed that "casting upon the waters" the outcomes of this Conference in the hope that the schools will quickly recognize the importance of population and family planning programs is not enough. There is a clear difference between a call to action and a program for action. The former is often unheeded because the program never materializes.

Obviously, some active committee or committees, international in composition, need to give immediate and serious attention to such matters as curriculum guides and teaching aids which will assist social work faculty members in developing family planning and population content in their schools. Furthermore, such faculty members need to be brought together periodically in conferences to share their experiences and to receive recent authoritative information from specialists in the population and family planning fields. Short-term training programs may also be required if the faculty members are to approach their new tasks with confidence.

While much emphasis needs to be placed upon helping U.S. schools of social work move ahead, the follow-up programs should be cross-national in scope, providing opportunities for social work educators in many countries to participate in their development and to receive training in applying relevant content in their schools. This offers possibilities for experimentation with, and evaluation of, several kinds of pedagogical approaches, provided the group in charge carefully formulates its curriculum models and has the necessary financial and personnel resources to give them thorough tests in a variety of educational settings.

With or without an international project such as the one just suggested, the Conference directive to schools of social work seems clear: the administration and faculty need to confront these issues directly. Each will work out its own solutions, but the responsibility of including content on population and family planning as part of its educational program can no longer be dodged.

In terms of this directive, the major result of this Conference is not only the documentation which it provided but the fact that social work educators from many countries and different kinds of schools of social work could come together with people knowledgeable about population dynamics to explore their common concerns. And the flow of information was two-way: the physicians, nurses, educators, social scientists all got a clearer picture of the contributions that social workers could make to social policy determination and planning, to program administration, to direct services to individuals, groups, families, and communities, and to manpower development. For many social workers, the interchange of ideas with those in other fields not only provided much information but helped strengthen a sense of commitment to the task of making social work a more integral part of the efforts to deal with the social aspects of the population problem.

THE SOCIAL WORKER'S RESPONSIBILITY

An implicit question behind much of the discussion at the Hawaii Conference was: What is the social worker's responsibility for seeking increased participation in population and family planning programs? Admittedly, in most countries social work's involvement has been limited —either because of lack of social work interest or because other professionals already engaged in these programs wanted no interlopers in their domain. Admittedly, also, schools of social work have done relatively little to prepare their graduates for careers related to population and family planning. Granted that the schools are ready to expand in these areas, how does a profession legitimatize its movement into a new field? Of what does the responsibility consist? One can mention at least four ways that the responsibility might be implemented.

1. A National Population Policy

When a national government decides upon an avowed policy to affect some population characteristic (reduce infant mortality, reduce population growth, etc.) all of those in the society who can contribute to the achievement of that policy have an authorization to make their voices heard and to ask for a chance to participate. They even have an obligation when the policy seems particularly urgent.

One can think of few urgent policies today which lie within the province of only one or two professions. A much broader team is needed in the face of the complexities of the problem being attacked. This is why surveys of professional schools more and more stress the need for students to gain a broad interdisciplinary background and also to learn enough about allied professions to be able to work with them when the nature of the problem requires this.

A further consideration is the fact that many programs go through stages in their approach to problems. Some professions take the lead at one stage and others prove necessary at a different stage. Evidence from at least two or three countries represented at the Conference indicates that family planning programs that are added to the clinical technical aspects of family planning place a greater stress upon a client-centered, counseling approach. Should this be the case, then social work must necessarily be involved.

As national programs become clarified and gain broader acceptance, professional associations and individual practitioners gain increased acceptance themselves by being actively and publicly connected with these programs. There is a discernible bandwagon effect which becomes legitimate if the profession concerned actually takes steps to prepare itself to perform effectively in the role it claims. Mere token gestures eventually discredit the hangers-on.

2. Self-proclaimed Competence and Relevance

Even where there is no national population policy a professional field can recognize a national need for one. It can proclaim its readiness to work with other professions in meeting that need. At the national conventions of its practitioners it may pass resolutions and policy statements that commit it to action; it may organize groups to deal with the problem. Such public statements usually describe the competence of the profession to speak on the issue and assume leadership. Sometimes one outside the field finds it hard to determine whether the views and concern expressed are those of a small, well-organized, influential group or whether they truly represent a broad interest throughout the profession. In time, one gauges this by noting actual achievements.

Part of the purpose of the Hawaii Conference was to give social work educators and others a chance to think through the nature of their contribution to population policy and family planning programs. This could lead to a more precise statement of what their responsibility actually was or should be. Understandably, in view of social work involvement to date, the emphasis was more on what should or might be done than upon what it actually is.

3. An Appeal from Outside the Profession

A strong bias for social work taking on this responsibility lies in the request from those outside the profession that it join in the cause in some fitting way. This does not occur if those in charge of the programs consider themselves completely adequate to the task, feel threatened by the intrusion of another profession, or think that the bureaucratic problems created by an extension to another profession would negate the expected gains. In the case of population policy and family planning programs, a health department might think it administratively very complicated to work within an established social welfare agency in a given type of activity or vice versa. It might prefer to add any required social workers to its own staff rather than to deal with these professionals through a different organizational channel. Even so, by adding the social workers it is signalling to the social work field that it needs the kind of help that this field can provide.

Despite apparent difficulties of collaboration, the physicians, nurses, and public health educators at the Hawaii Conference welcomed the idea of social work contributions to family planning programs. They were a select, highly experienced collection of individuals who did not claim to speak for their profession as a whole, but their influence is considerable.

The day may very well come—particularly when social work has adequately prepared itself—that professions now in the forefront of population and family planning programs may not only be receptive to social work but may even put pressure upon it to handle aspects which it can cover better than any other field. When such a day arrives, the responsibility for social work will be secure.

4. The Record of Performance

In several countries represented at the Conference social workers have not been worrying about their responsibility; they simply went out to work in family planning programs at whatever tasks they considered themselves qualified to do. In Iran social workers recognized the need and moved to train people to deal with the population problem. Elsewhere, too, social workers have demonstrated the ability to assume the responsibility and are recognized as essential to successful programs. Such performance hastens the acceptance of social work by other professions and leads to the request for even greater assistance; it lends greater credence to any self-proclaimed assumption of responsibility emanating from the field; and it demonstrates social work's concern about a major social problem.

Again, though, we face the bottleneck to performance: namely, adequately trained social workers who can join with other professionals but at the same time make a unique contribution on their own. A few gifted individuals can always provide examples of what might be done, but the profession cannot be said to be carrying out its share of responsibility until the rank and file in the profession are sensitive to the issues and can make some contribution in the course of their regular job, and until some practitioners decide to make population policy and family planning a career specialty.

PART II :
Conference Papers

A World-Wide View of a Universal Problem[1]

MILOS MACURA

Over-impressed by recent developments in such spectacular areas as nuclear energy, computers, and space, we too often neglect to address ourselves to the imperfection of human knowledge. This neglect restricts imagination, thinking, and action as we approach the end of the twentieth century. Surprisingly enough, those aspects of human life, behavior, and activity which are the most intimate to man, going back to the beginning of his history, suffer more from incomplete knowledge and inadequate action than the ones that have emerged more recently. Perhaps the former are more complex as they deal with man and his many facets; perhaps there is a lack of self-examination and self-understanding.

The population problem is by all means one of the crucial aspects of human life affected by lack of knowledge and neglect. Is the population problem, however, really "affected by lack of knowledge and neglect"? Instead of answering this question, it may be pertinent to raise a few questions concerning our knowledge, vision, and action.

How much do we know of reproductive behavior, of reproductive physiology, or of why fertility levels and patterns differ from one group to another or from one society to another? What are the mechanics of individual aspects of the unique process of human reproduction? To what

[1] The views expressed in this paper are those of the author and do not necessarily reflect the opinions of the United Nations.

Milos Macura is director of the Population Division of the United Nations.

extent does existing knowledge contribute to the solution of the problem? How much are the humanistic, aesthetic, ethical, and religious ingredients of the population problem enlightened by philosophy, religion, and arts? Is the population problem really less important for humanity than human dignity, human rights, freedom, war and peace, or space?

Does the awareness of demographic effects influence the individuals' decisions concerning the size of his family? How many people, particularly among the underprivileged classes and in the economically advanced nations, can decide and do decide on the number of their children? How many governments have adopted a policy aimed at assisting parents in making this most critical decision? How effective are governments in this respect?

If the answers to these questions are rather on the negative side and therefore disappointing—as they definitely are—they only reflect the current state of affairs. It is true that the last decade has witnessed significant developments in awareness, knowledge, and policies concerning population, and that at the beginning of the current decade the world is more population-conscious than it ever was. However, in comparison with the magnitude of the problem, the progress achieved so far is far from satisfactory.

THE ORIGIN OF THE PROBLEM

To say that the population problem is specific to the second part of the twentieth century and to reduce it to excessive fertility only is both erroneous and misleading. Population problems have existed and will perhaps continue to exist, owing either to unfavorable demographic processes or to maladjustment of economic structures and institutions, or a combination of both.

Throughout history and until the nineteenth century what we regarded as major population problems were high fertility accompanied by high mortality and a low expectancy of life span determined by hostile environment, poor economic conditions, and defective social order. No significant demographic differences existed between what are currently termed "less developed" and "more developed" regions. The rate of population growth was rather low in both regions, at an average of around 0.5 percent per annum. Change in population trends was perhaps incidental with mortality as the dynamic factor, influenced by poor harvests, epidemics, and other calamities.

In the regions now considered more advanced, the nineteenth century gradually brought about a demographic revolution. Rapid declines in mortality rates were followed, after a lag, by declines in fertility. However, the population growth rate reached an unprecedented high level of 1.2 percent per annum. In some regions and during some periods it reached 1.5 percent per annum. Growing numbers of working-age population provided ample labor for expanding and diversified industries. Demographic change was a self-induced, long-lasting, and painful process, involving profound modification in human behavior, employment, and settlement, as well as uneasy social adjustment. Improvements in health were slow and gradual, control of fertility was difficult and occasionally brutal, migrations (both urban–rural and overseas) were hard, and all these combined with the given economic and social circumstances created a variety of population problems.

No spectacular change in population trends occurred in the less developed regions until the late 1950s. The coincidence of demographic change with the change in the political setting in the less developed regions that established new independent and sovereign nations is apparent, but the relation between the two phenomena is obscure. We definitely know, however, that the downward mortality trend already observed in some regions in the late 1930s suddenly accelerated after the Second World War, with a significant extension of life expectancy as a consequence. On the other hand, the fertility rate remained high and even increased in some areas due to improvement in health conditions and nutrition, which tended to reduce miscarriages and secondary sterility. The results are now obvious and well-known: during the last twenty-five years, rates of population growth have almost doubled in the less developed regions. However, this process of accelerated population growth remained little noticed for many years.

The demographic change which the less developed regions are currently undergoing was induced by their health policy and facilitated by the progress made in medicine and sanitary technology in the developed countries. It gave rise to new population problems of both a demographic and socio-economic nature. Disproportion between fertility and mortality, a very high population growth, an excessively young age structure, and the fast growth of urban population combined with massive increases in rural population are only a few examples of the former. The essentially socio-economic problems include food crises, unemployment, inadequate educational facilities, slums, social conflicts and tensions, lack of housing, environmental problems, etc. It is significant that all these manifestations of the population problem have persisted in spite of economic and social progress, which was not commensurate with population change. It is also significant that almost all components of population problems are influenced by a common phenomenon, that is, the disproportion between fertility and mortality trends.

THE MAGNITUDE OF THE PROBLEM

A brief summary of a complex problem tends always to oversimplification and vulgarization, which may also be true for the present summary. In order to avoid misunderstanding a few statistics will be given.

According to Durand's estimate the world population was about 750 million in 1750 and about 1,650 million in the year 1900. The United Nations estimated the world population for 1965 at about 3,280 million, and by the year 2000 it may reach 6,500 million. The first doubling of population since 1750 took about 150 years, the second about 65 years, and the third may not take more than 35 years. The absolute increase in world population during the 150 years of the first period was 900 million; during the second period of 65 years it was 1,630 million; during the third or current period of 35 years it may exceed 3,000 million. During this most critical period the increase in the population of the less developed regions may well surpass 2,500 million.

The past two centuries of accelerated population growth of the world already belong to history. It is indeed good to learn and know about them in order to understand better the kind of combinations of political, economic, social, and demographic circumstances which have brought the population problem to the present magnitude. But this historical experience cannot provide either technical competence or guidance—at least within the reach of existing knowledge or sound imagination—which could immediately alleviate the current difficult situation or make it possible to foresee short-term and rapid improvements in the inherited momentum of population trends.

We should therefore concentrate upon the future and try to visualize the trends and possible changes in the demographic-social-economic complex, and then attempt to identify those areas of immediate and prospective action which are of particular interest to this Conference. Perhaps the suggestions made for the United Nations Second Development Decade can serve as a background for the foregoing discussion. A rather impressive rate of economic growth has been suggested for the 1970s—6 to 7 percent per annum—which may induce or accelerate change in many vital areas of social life and institutions of the less developed world, which, in turn, may decelerate population growth. Demographic projections prepared for the decade are not optimistic, however, because of the momentum of population growth. They anticipate a very rapid expansion of population, with massive increases in the number of people in the less developed areas and significant structural changes which will not be easy to manage.

The medium variant of the United Nations projections prepared for the Second Development Decade anticipates two different patterns of population growth in the more and the less developed regions of the world. For the sake of a better understanding of the trends during the 1970s, the estimates are extended until the year 1985.

	More Developed Regions				**Less Developed Regions**			
Years	**1965/70**	**70/75**	**75/80**	**80/85**	**1965/70**	**70/75**	**75/80**	**80/85**
Rate of growth (per 100)	1.0	1.0	1.1	1.1	2.4	2.5	2.4	2.4
Crude birth rate (per 1000)	18.6	18.9	19.5	19.5	40.6	39.0	37.0	34.9
Gross reproduction rate	1.3	1.3	1.3	1.3	2.8	2.7	2.6	2.4
Crude death rate (per 1000)	9.1	9.2	9.3	9.4	16.1	14.2	12.5	10.9
Expectancy of life at birth (years)	70.4	71.2	71.9	72.2	49.5	52.4	55.3	58.0

For the more developed regions, a constant reproduction rate, a slight increase in the crude birth rate due to the change in age structure combined with a further extension of life expectancy, and a slight increase in the crude death rate owing to the aging process may be expected to result in a constant moderate rate of growth of population. On the other hand, the population of the combined less developed regions may be expected to grow at the same high rate as in the recent past as a result of declining birth and reproduction rates, the effects of which may be offset by further substantial reduction of death rates accompanied by prolongation of the life span.

Reproductive patterns of individual populations may and will differ, as will their economic and social determinants. Manifestations of population problems and their socio-economic implications will range widely in substance and intensity and consequently will call for diversified policy measures. But if all national and sub-national peculiarities may be at this stage forgotten, we may anticipate a world population fifteen years from now of 4,900 million, or 1,300 million more people than in 1970. Inhabitants of the less developed regions may exceed 3,600 million, while in the more developed ones the total may reach nearly 1,300 million.

MACRO IMPLICATIONS OF POPULATION TRENDS

Tremendous efforts, unprecedented mobilization of resources, far better knowledge, and more efficient organization will be needed to manage the potentials and desires arising from anticipated population trends. In order to achieve modest economic improvements in the less developed regions in both aggregate and *per capita* terms, involvement of and action by individuals, nations, and the world community is essential.

It is, of course, difficult and even impossible to summarize all the varied and diverse requirements and potentialities that originate in population trends and structures. This is among the most difficult tasks in anticipating social advancement and economic development at the national level. It is a much more difficult task if only a dichotomized world is considered, that is, if one distinguishes only between the more developed and the less developed regions. However, with all the difficulties in mind and with the hope that imagination may help in translating dry data and flat projections into real-life categories, the following may be suggested for the next fifteen years. It should be pointed out that all data concern only the additions to individual population contingents over the next fifteen years, while in actual fact provisions should be made for both the additional requirements and the improvements that are needed in view of the unsatisfactory current state of affairs.

Thus, during the next fifteen years only, from 1970 to 1985, additional provision should be made for:

1. Food, housing, clothing, and other essentials for 1,117 million additional people (or 44 percent more in 1985 than in 1970) in the less developed regions and 184 million (or 17 percent) in the more developed regions;
2. Employment in order to utilize the productive capacity of an additional 660 million people of working age (47 percent more) in the less developed regions, and 115 million in the more developed ones (17 percent more);
3. Improvement of prospects and opportunities for 217 million additional youth (or 45 percent more than in 1970) in the less developed regions, and 13 million (an additional 7 percent) in the more developed ones;
4. Basic education for an additional school-age population of 273 million (43 percent more) in the less developed and 20 million (or 10 percent) in the more developed regions;
5. Child care for 131 million new young children (32 percent) in the less developed regions and 22 million (24 percent) in the more developed ones;

6. Security and protection for a significant percentage of 53 million people aged 65 years and over in the less developed regions (an increase of 63 percent) and 27 million people in the more developed regions (26 percent increase);

7. Education and services needed to control pregnancy and birth for 248 million more women of reproductive age (46 percent more than in 1970) in the less developed regions and for a portion of 31 million women in the more developed regions;

8. Space and facilities needed for an additional 537 million urban population (84 percent more) in the less developed regions and for 258 million (or 36 percent) in the more developed regions;

9. Agricultural land, employment, and housing for a new rural population of 549 million (30 percent increase) in the less developed regions.

Considering the demographic projections, we may conclude that there is a high probability that man in the more developed regions will, in 1985, still struggle for fresh air and clean water and fight against pollution, urban crises, and congestion because of rapid growth of urban population and the difficulties of managing the environment. Following this would be the problem of old age and security combined with the health problems of elderly people. The anticipated increase in the child population and in the population of working age perhaps would not create additional problems, although some employment problems would undoubtedly persist as a consequence of inequalities in income distribution and in regional development. The rather moderate growth of the female population of reproductive age would tend to keep the fertility rate at a moderate level, except that it may be higher among the poor classes and in disadvantaged areas. The projected growth of the youth population is very moderate and would suggest that there would be no demographic reasons around 1985 for youth discontent. This, however, does not exclude the possibility of other social and political reasons for discontent.

On further consideration of the same projections, it seems almost certain that the man of the less developed regions would have to make tremendous efforts to overcome the many-sided problems imposed by the high growth of total population and of all its significant component groups. His task would be much more difficult than it is now, for he would still be faced with the unfavorable composition of productive factors combined with high population growth and large additional numbers of people. There is hope that food and agricultural production would not be an insurmountable problem due to the "green revolution" and its foreseeable prospects. However, massive increases in rural population and growing agricultural overpopulation may be a limiting factor which might provoke a slowing down of agricultural progress and create agrarian tensions. While rapid growth rates are foreseen for the old-age population, the provision of necessary care for this group would not create special difficulties since the group is rather small and the intra-family security system could still be expected to prevail in large sections of society. Serious problems would also accompany the great expansion of urban population, and it seems likely that slums, overcrowding, and unhealthy living conditions would be difficult to overcome around 1985.

Rapid and massive increases in the female population of reproductive age in combination with prevailing high fertility levels will clearly be the dominant population problem with long-range demographic and socioeconomic implications. Educating the women entering reproductive age and influencing reproductive behavior and motivation, as well as provision of facilities for regulating fertility, would also be enormous tasks and not easy to solve.

The second item of importance is likely to be the provision of employment opportunity in view of large increments in the labor force, not to mention the serious backlog in unemployment and underemployment and the lack of capital and skill. Many economic and social issues would continue to cluster around productivity, income distribution, and, consequently, the level of living, which would, in the final analysis, also depend on the size of the family. The pressure of school-age population on schools and out-of-school educational facilities would significantly increase, and the problems of providing adequate opportunities for the growing numbers of youth would intensify.

It should be pointed out that problems arising from the rapid population growth are not the only demographic problems which need concern the less developed regions. Despite the remarkable progress which has been made in controlling mortality, death rates in infancy and early childhood and maternal mortality will remain high in many less developed regions and will continue to create serious problems at both individual and demographic levels.

The preceding analysis underlines the necessity for meeting the growing requirements of increasing population, particularly in the less developed regions, and insists on rapid economic development and social amelioration. It also emphasizes the crucial role of rapidly growing population in creating additional demands which the economically active population cannot easily supply owing to inadequate factors of production. This means that under conditions of abundant population supply and scarce natural resources and capital, the satisfaction of all kinds of requirements would be easier if population growth and its annual increments were smaller. This is perhaps the most crucial factor in the demographic consideration of the future development of the world and of the less developed regions, a factor which suggests that among a range of policies and measures affecting population those which influence its growth be given the highest priority.

GOVERNMENT POLICIES

It is perhaps correct to state that all modern governments, irrespective of the stage of advancement of the nation, design policies and launch economic and social measures which influence the progress of individual socio-economic groups of population and the geographical distribution of population. There is not one government among a group of about 130 sovereign nations which has not established a policy aimed at improving health conditions, extending longevity, and combating mortality. There are, however, only 30 governments which have adopted policies designed to moderate family size and composition, rationalize and humanize reproduction, and moderate fertility. It is surprising but true that the two respective policies, both of which affect family size and population growth, were not pursued simultaneously until 1951, when India upgraded the idea of fertility control to a government policy level.

From 1950 to 1959 four governments of developing nations adopted fertility control as a national policy and developed government programs known as "national family planning programs." From 1960 to 1964 six additional governments, and from 1965 to 1969 about eighteen more governments, introduced their own policies, in addition to which there were not less than five countries in which family planning was declared a policy of the Ministry of Health. A number of other governments have recently liberalized previously restrictive laws concerning fertility regulation. Still another group of governments, with varying degrees of official involvement, either actively support or tolerate the family planning services provided by voluntary organizations. There is also a group of governments who have not taken any official position so far or who disapprove of official involvement in fertility regulation.

Established policies differ both in respect to demographic objectives and motives. While many governments organize family planning services with a view to moderating fertility and population growth, some governments have no demographic targets and a few governments even favor a larger population. No policy has as an objective an optimum size and composition of population which would tend to reconcile individual and national aspirations. Motives for adopting a policy generally emphasize humanistic objections but are also directed at eradicating demographic or social malformations. This is perhaps a sign of the imperfection and underdevelopment of the twentieth-century societies whose policy decisions are focused on eliminating inherited and newly created inadequacies rather than on achieving optimal situations.

The group of countries with an established governmental policy is both representative and impressive. It includes many countries, irrespective of their levels of economic development, size, cultural background, race and ethnic origin, religion and beliefs, social organization, or political systems. In the less developed areas of the world it extends to countries whose combined population comprises over 700 percent of the total in these areas, although not all people of reproductive age are as yet benefiting from the programs.

The increasing acceptance of policies designed at regulating fertility or promoting family planning and the diversity of countries with such policies are indicative of a process similar to the processes which have taken place a decade or so ago, when many governments adopted significant reforms. This process has been reflected in the respective organizations of the United Nations system, all of which, since 1965, have established their own policies concerning population in general and fertility regulation in particular. It is expected that the developments already started will progress and that the 1970s will bring additional countries and additional considerations into population policymaking.

A large spectrum of economic, social, ideological, and ethical considerations underlie official population policies with emphasis on population or human welfare, depending upon national circumstances. The two basic approaches are indeed not mutually exclusive, for they reflect two different sides of a single phenomenon—human fertility. In promoting or approving the small family size norm which, under conditions of low mortality, is directly related to low fertility and consequently to slow population growth, governments are motivated by a number of factors. For the purpose of the present discussion, these factors may be classified under five headings: socio-economic, family welfare, well-being and health of individuals, human rights and dignity, and moral considerations. Perhaps a sixth factor may be added—the rationale of reproduction.

The detrimental effect of high population growth in respect to economic and social progress are perhaps the main reasons for the growing concern over advancement of the less developed regions. An impressive stock of research and literature supports the proposition that a high population rate adversely affects saving and investment, technological progress and employment, and consumption and social services through the heavy pressure of population upon resources and the unsatisfactory economic and demographic structures. Although largely adopted, this proposition is, on the other hand, questioned in some developing countries on the grounds of ample natural resources and on the theory that existing social institutions and political settings do not favor rapid economic expansion. The principle of equal opportunity, over-urbanization, responsibility of the society for the family, and general social advancement are also among the macro-social considerations favoring population control. It should be pointed out that no government or international organization favors population control as a substitute for economic development and social progress; all three are viewed as complementary and mutually supporting with the framework of an overall transformation of less advanced societies.

The concept of family welfare as promoted by family planning is closely related to the small-size family as a modern pattern. It seems to be both a condition for and a consequence of low fertility and low mortality of infants. Living conditions, in the broadest sense, are among the major preoccupations in this context, while intra-family relations and relations between generations are apparently neglected.

Two specific groups of individuals—mothers and children—are the center of interest of birth control programs for both ethical and social reasons. The deliberate spacing of children is favored because it eliminates a high incidence of maternal or infant mortality, minimizes the health hazards of continuous childbearing, and promotes childcare and puericulture. In many societies the eradication of criminal abortion as well as the treatment of sterility and infertility which is a part of family planning programs, is an important contribution to female health. While the protection of the mother emphasizes the health aspects, the protection of the child from the harmful effects of excessive fertility also involves social considerations such as better education and brighter prospects for the future.

Family planning as a matter of human right and dignity is a rather complex concept. In addition to the status of women, which is an early proposition for a moderate fertility compatible with the modern role of women in society, it also includes the rights of parents to decide upon the number of their children and to have access to information and services needed to implement their decision. Both the concepts of the status of women and the right of parents imply human dignity and propound that educated and responsible individuals will make adequate decisions with respect to the size of their families. A more recent proposition concerns the rights of children, which, in the final analysis, suggests that the size of the family be adjusted to its capability of bringing up and educating children.

Ethical considerations are implied in more than one proposition underlying fertility control discussed so far, since many of them deal primarily with humanistic and social aspects. Another concept—conscientious and responsible parenthood—is perhaps a more ethic-oriented concept than the planned parenthood concept, although both underline the role and responsibilities of parents *vis-à-vis* their children. This is also a micro concept concerned with individuals and their specific role in the family.

What has been considered above has only an indirect relation to the meaning and quality of the reproductive process as a demographic phenomenon. The question of "what is the rationale of human reproduction from the point of view of demography" seems, therefore, quite appropriate. "Continuation of the human species" is the obvious answer, but with no further qualification. Because of voluntary control of fertility and low mortality, continuation of the species may be guided by different criteria. Since the economic and social functions of the human beings who constitute a population are the major discriminating features of human populations, we should perhaps be looking for rational and humane reproduction.

MICRO ASPECTS EMPHASIZED

Because it is an aggregate of individual births, fertility as a demographic phenomenon (which, together with mortality, determines population growth) depends upon millions of decisions, or the lack of millions of decisions on the part of individuals. The growth, and consequently the size, of population is an outcome of a spontaneous process, the participants in which are not aware of the result and its implications. The reproduction of population is definitely the most decentralized human activity and perhaps the most difficult to control and influence.

Government policy aimed at lowering fertility may therefore be successful only to the extent that popular support permits. This means that emphasis is not only on the macro level, the level of the government, which is indeed very important, but also on the micro level, the level of the individual and the family. This is probably the main limiting factor of government action affecting fertility.

Underlining the two levels (macro and micro) alone is not fully justified, for there is an intermediate level at which reproductive behavior and motivation are shaped. At this level, cultural values, norms, beliefs, and prejudices operate through informal or formal groups and institutions to press upon the individual's decision-making process and to influence the level and pattern of demographic fertility. For the sake of convenience, however, the intermediate level may be considered a part of the micro level.

Having pointed out that the decisive factor in fertility control is the individual and his family, two additional comments seem pertinent. First, the population policies of governments rightly insist on family welfare and the well-being of the individual. Second, governments should give the most considered attention to the education of individuals and parents in order to induce progressive change which would be, *inter alia,* favorable to the small family norm.

Indeed, this is not an easy task; it involves demographic diagnosis, the delicate and subtle matters involved in many aspects of individual and family life, and contraceptive technology. A number of disciplines and a variety of expertise are needed for both the understanding of problems and the action to be taken on them. These needs range from demography, home economics, and agricultural extension through health and pediatrics, to social psychology, motivation, and social work. Yet they all have to be integrated in approach and action at ground level in order to induce a change in the family compatible with national development and individual aspirations.

If deliberate fertility control at both demographic and individual levels could be envisaged as a circuit, the elements of which were demography, government policy, contraceptive technology, and social action, we could perhaps try to answer (for operational purposes only, of course) the questions which were raised in the introductory comments.

Far better demographic statistics and more sensitive and sophisticated analyses are needed immediately in order to facilitate the implementation of policies aiming at a balanced, if not optimum demographic situation. In addition to action promoted by family planning programs, governmental measures need to take advantage of the interplay of demographic and socio-economic factors in a developmental process to encourage and speed up demographic changes. Family planning services, irrespective of the development of better birth control methods, urgently require substantial improvements and extension. Also requiring special attention are the education of people and the creation of an awareness of inter-relatedness between family size and improvement in living conditions. This is a real challenge to social research, social work, and social work education, all of which play an increasing role in family planning programs as integral parts of overall national development.

Social Work Roles and Opportunities for Service[1]

AIDA GINDY

Social work education stands today at the crossroads facing challenges of a new decade which will deeply influence social welfare policies, planning, and programming. We have entered a decade which has been internationally pronounced as the second development decade promising social justice, human development, and a level of adequate living for the greatest majority of the population. It promises a generous social investment in education, health, housing, family welfare, nutrition, and other social components necessary to raise levels of living in correspondence to investments for economic development.

In addressing itself to population dynamics, population policies, and family planning, this Conference opens a challenging new area of service to social workers. Both the developed and the developing countries acknowledge that the profession of social work is still at the threshold of a potentially far-reaching contribution when it deals with the issue of population dynamics. The role of the social worker has to be understood more clearly and schools of social work have just started to think about strengthening their educational offerings in this area. While it is generally recognized that the social worker has a strategic and crucial role to play, the exact nature of the contribution is not understood or accepted in a like measure in all the countries by all sectors of development.

[1] The views expressed in this paper are those of the author and do not necessarily reflect the views of the United Nations.

Aida Gindy is chief of the Social Welfare Services Section, Social Development Division of the United Nations.

The social work contribution to population policies and national family planning programs has numerous and varied aspects. Some countries see the role of the social worker in the area of research, planning, and policymaking. Others see the social worker functioning primarily as a practitioner within the context of family and child welfare. A few countries have put their emphasis on training high-level specialized workers. Several more countries strongly press the need for auxiliary front-line workers who are more involved in motivational programs. A considerable number see the social worker's role as part of an interdisciplinary team approach.

Population programs and the place of social welfare in them may be considered at two levels:

1. The activities at a "macro" level which contribute to the control of population and to the development and implementation of policies which increase living standards and promote several aspects of welfare. Such policy aspects may include housing, education, employment, and other welfare services which research has shown to have a favorable impact in reducing fertility trends and the need to have large families.
2. Those activities at a "micro" level which contribute directly to meeting those needs associated with family planning such as counseling, changing community attitudes toward large families, and other barriers to the acceptance of family-limiting services.

It must be stressed that the micro-level activities are as crucial as those at the macro level. Both are equally important roles which must go together for a basically sound policy of population planning. Social welfare personnel are needed for discharging these two complementary roles in any country's program which has been carefully planned in relation to the country's needs, resources, socio-cultural background, and future development.

Keeping the above distinctions in mind, we can highlight the roles of social workers in family planning programs as follows:

1. CONTRIBUTION TO FAMILY PLANNING, RESEARCH, POLICIES, AND NATIONAL PLANS

In the developing regions of the world, the need for incorporation of the social welfare component in national research on family planning policies, plans, and programs is increasingly felt. With more emphasis on the developmental functions of social welfare, there is a pressing parallel demand for greater involvement of the social welfare leadership in formulating national family planning programs. In this context, social work contributes indirectly to the overall comprehensive policies guiding and directing national family planning policies. There is a need, therefore, among social welfare leadership for knowledge about population dynamics —knowledge such as the pace of migration of people from rural to urban areas, fertility trends, and population projections.

Social welfare researchers have technical expertise to contribute to the comprehensive research which determines national population policies and plans. Among the expected contributions are studies on attitudinal changes, family size and patterns, size and structures of families and households, the relation of different types of family unions to fertility levels, husband-wife relationships, and attitudes to children. Other major areas include research affecting the youth population, for example, attitudes toward sex, unmarried mothers, and the needs associated with the growing numbers of unmarried mothers such as employment, education, social aspirations, and justice. More research is required on the new functions and roles of family and child welfare services in the implementation of family planning programs; there is also a need to assess the contribution of social welfare personnel at all levels for participation in family planning programs. Some may question why these fields of research, which are already well cultivated by sociologists, anthropologists, psychologists, and others in allied disciplines, should be of particular interest to social welfare personnel, social workers, and social work educators. The answer lies in the social worker's unique knowledge of the individual, his human behavior, feelings, values, attitudes, anxieties, and family relationships—all of which are major factors underlying any social research carried out in the field of family planning.

Let us now look at the special contribution of social welfare and the social worker in policymaking. In comprehensive social planning, there are two aspects to be considered: (1) the policymaking and planning activities that lead to higher living standards and economic growth which helps reduce the birth rate, and (2) policymaking specifically within the area of family planning in relation to other aspects of social planning. In the first area, social welfare personnel can contribute to areas related to policies influencing income distribution, employment, housing, industrialization, and other related areas which are outside the scope of this paper. In connection with policymaking specifically within the area of family planning, social welfare leadership should be called upon to contribute more concretely and constructively to national plans affecting family planning and population policies.

The contribution social welfare personnel can bring to overall planning is derived from their knowledge of the needs and aspirations of the people and their skills applied in enlisting active popular support for development efforts. Social welfare practitioners can bring to the attention of the planners their accumulated knowledge of problems regarding development and utilization of human resources, attitudes of individuals and families inimical to changes, and individual or group reactions to economic incentives.

2. THE SOCIAL WORKER AS PRACTITIONER: CONTRIBUTION TO ATTITUDINAL CHANGE

The direct contribution the social worker can make to family planning is centered primarily on his attributes and skills as a practitioner. By virtue of their profession, social welfare personnel are human relations specialists and are involved in the daily lives of individuals, families, and communities at large. They are aware of the culture, mores, traditions, and taboos influencing family lives. They are familiar with family motivations, attitudes, reactions, and potentialities. They are qualified to advise on intimate areas of social relationships, psychological problems, and cultural inhibitions and values that have a direct bearing on the success or failure of population planning programs.

In considering the contribution of social workers, attention must also be given to the services extended by the professional worker, the intermediate-level worker, and the volunteer.

Professional Social Worker

Social workers who have had advanced training in social work on a university level or its equivalent are still few in numbers. Those social workers who have studied beyond a bachelor's degree or its equivalent, such as in North America, are becoming more consciously involved in population programs and family planning activities. They have been primarily involved in training programs and supervisory responsibility for auxiliary social workers. A very modest number have been involved in overall family planning research and policymaking and planning of comprehensive population programs.

Professional social workers as practitioners make their contribution more directly to family planning programs within the frame of traditional medico-social services, for example, maternal and child health centers, family social services centers, hospital maternity wards, birth control clinics, public health departments, welfare departments. The services of these social workers center primarily on family counseling, parents' education, and family life education. They provide individualized services focused on the social and psychological aspects of family planning programs. They counsel parents, individually and together, on family limiting programs; they provide factual information, help with problem clarification, and assist with effective referrals for family planning services.

The competence of professional group workers has been increasingly used in direct services related to family planning programs. They deal with groups of clients who share common problems and concerns. They can lead discussion groups which are educational and informational in nature and which clarify problems, fears, and misconceptions expressed and conveyed by members of the group.

The role of youth in national development has been receiving urgent attention by social welfare policymakers, administrators, and practitioners. The problems and needs of young people in the developing world, where half of the population is under twenty-five years of age, are receiving necessary attention. Social welfare personnel in the developed countries have begun to give equal attention to the need to counsel and advise young people on family planning. Group workers have important roles to play with informal group meetings of young people who may wish to express their own feelings and anxieties about family planning practices. The attitudes of young people regarding the social acceptability of different contraceptive methods and their views on such matters as marriage and family life, incomplete families, and unmarried couples provide an important source of knowledge for social welfare personnel.

In some developing countries, where over-population has not yet emerged as an urgent national problem, social welfare personnel in family planning centers work with clients on problems related to sterility, spacing of children, and family life education. In these circumstances, as in those concerned with limiting family size, the social worker carries the same role. Basic principles and skills are applied to enable individuals to make the final choice, based on personal conviction and family needs, in deciding whether or not to utilize the family planning facilities.

The community organization worker is involved primarily in interdisciplinary teamwork, contributing to concerted planning on a community or national level. Serving as catalysts for community action programs, community organizers help citizen groups on a village or urban level to draw up their own programs based on expressed interest and mutual help. They serve as resource counselors to community groups and can be effective in changing attitudes and promoting social action.

Whatever the methodology employed by social workers—casework, group work, or community organization—an urgent need for generalists who can use a variety of methods has emerged, particularly in the developing countries.

The Intermediate-Level Social Worker

In a number of developing countries, there are still relatively few professional social workers who have received advanced training abroad. They are employed primarily in urban areas with responsibility for supervisory, training, and administrative posts. This has opened the door wide to the intermediate-level worker who, in many countries, carries the professional tasks. This category of social worker—particularly in the developing world—has been assigned to generic social welfare responsibilities which cut across a number of development problems.

From the modest information available on the involvement of social welfare personnel in family planning programs, it is generally observed that in the developing countries the intermediate social worker plays an important role. It is in those countries where community development programs have been effective that the intermediate-level social workers, together with auxiliary personnel, have been most closely allied with group activities and motivational action programs. For example, it was observed in the United Arab Republic that the female village-level social workers, who are recruited from the villages in which they serve, have helped the women of the villages to discuss the methods and practices of family planning more openly in group meetings. The social worker's role in this context included problem clarification through discussion and the offer of complementary services, such as factual information about family planning services and provision of transport to attend family planning clinics. The Ministry of Social Welfare helped to train the intermediate-level social workers and has assessed the impact of their services. It has been reported that these village workers proved to be more successful in motivating their own communities than specialized social workers who, although highly trained, were not always able to communicate with the unsophisticated village women.

A very important skill that a social worker learns to use, whether at the middle-level or as a community development worker in rural settings, is how to motivate and train volunteers to contribute to social change through family planning programs. For example, Ghana, India, Kenya, Pakistan, and Tunisia, through their national rural women's programs, have used volunteers who personally undertook home visits and counseling in their respective communities.

These are ways in which intermediate-level social welfare personnel carry out professional responsibilities and serve as catalysts for attitudinal change. They have studied their communities, assessed the community leadership resources, and dealt with citizen groups sharing the same objectives and concern. Social welfare personnel, whatever their titles, have endeavored to carry out the developmental social welfare functions which contribute to the overall objectives of population policies. The social worker as a practitioner regards family planning as an aspect of total family life which includes the welfare of children. Intermediate social welfare personnel or auxiliary workers have often been trained for multipurpose tasks. This has helped them to become more readily involved as generalists using all basic social work methods in responding to the needs of the community they serve.

Volunteers

Volunteers are a rich resource whose services can be effectively mobilized for motivational and attitudinal change. Citizens' committees, women's movements, women's clubs, parents' groups, and youth groups are all indigenous potential resource groups whose members, if trained, could have a positive, direct impact on population programs. This has already been demonstrated in Iran, Pakistan, Kenya, Ghana, and Tunisia where volunteers, particularly members of women's groups, have provided a task force for educational programs. In many cases the way has been prepared for a sympathetic group to serve as interpreters of national family planning programs and a means of communication for local groups. In some instances such groups have had direct influence on national policies and programs.

A special effort has been made in a number of developing countries to work with women's groups and women's organizations in family planning programs. In the countries of North Africa, the *assistantes sociales* or *aides sociaux* (auxiliary workers) have been closely allied to national women's organizations. Emphasis has been placed on family life education, preparation of women for family responsibilities, spacing of children, and child development. Development of women's programs, which formerly essentially stressed education for home life and family life, now extend to education and training for responsibilities in community action and national development. Women's clubs, citizen groups, and social action groups have provided strong leadership in the interpretation and promotion of family planning programs. Social welfare personnel active in community development have become more involved in programs related to the advancement of women. Intermediate-level social workers have also become increasingly involved in programs related to the changing status of women, marriage laws, women's attitudes to changes in family patterns, attitudes toward contraception and birth control, and legislation affecting abortion and sterilization.

Volunteers can carry out a number of functions or tasks which the trained social worker is not always available to perform. Volunteer leaders with a knowledge of the local community and sensitivity to its changing needs can assist in group education and community action and can bring about community support based on principles of mutual help. Adequate provision should be made for the training and supervision of such personnel so that their special contribution can be made to fit in an important way into national social development programs.

3. SOCIAL WELFARE PERSONNEL AS MEMBERS OF INTERDISCIPLINARY TEAMS

Social workers no longer work in isolation. With their involvement in the broad objectives of national development, they face the challenge of working in closer coordination with allied professions.

Interdisciplinary relationships take various forms. First, there is the cooperative relationship among different professionals engaged in implementing sectoral objectives, for example, psychologists and teachers in education; nutritionists and child care specialists in home economics; economists, sociologists, anthropologists, and family welfare personnel in family planning research centers. This is in the nature of a helping relationship among the different sectors so that there is no duplication, conflict, or absence of services. Second, there is the relationship in which each discipline works to integrate parts of a whole program meaningfully so that one measure reinforces or complements another. Thus, a welfare worker may learn how to teach better health habits or a health worker may find out how to promote better social relationships within the family. The two workers learn to make their knowledge areas and skills complementary in reinforcing overall objectives.

To encompass the overwhelming tasks of development, a particular type of interdisciplinary approach has been adopted, primarily at the level of the intermediate worker, to strengthen social welfare training programs. Sometimes social welfare training is combined with nursing, midwifery, and home economics. Such training programs are provided for "social aides" in French-speaking African countries. In a number of English-speaking countries, training for intermediate-level workers in community development has emphasized social work methodology in combination with adult education and agriculture. An integrated health and welfare approach has proved particularly helpful in socio-medical programs, particularly those now related to family planning.

In a number of French-speaking African countries, maternal and child welfare health centers have provided a nucleus for the well-being of children, women, and other family members. They make available services to improve the nutrition of expectant mothers and young children, to advise women on family planning and spacing of children, and to give information on contraception. These centers depend on social welfare personnel for family counseling, parent education, provision of day-care services, and enlisting community support for attitudinal change.

In a recent United Nations' evaluation of family planning programs in Pakistan, the report concluded that "family planning officers and local organizers will be called upon increasingly to play . . . the role of health and welfare workers"[2] because in the last analysis family planning means social change. The provision of extension services that offer a multiple approach to family planning by relating it to health, maternal and child welfare, vocational guidance, etc., has proved to be an effective channel of adult education and a means of promoting social change.

Related to the question of an interdisciplinary approach is the larger question of integrating several disciplines in a single training program and in field activities for a meaningful discharge of social welfare functions. Is there any scope for integrated training as a way to find new solutions to current problems? If such development takes place, what possibilities are there for re-orienting the programs of some of the training institutions in the field of social work?

4. ROLE OF SOCIAL WORK TRAINING INSTITUTIONS

Training institutions responsible for social work education are currently undergoing a complex but challenging change. As welfare objectives are seen increasingly as part and parcel of national development, the accent on governmental tasks calls for new approaches and emphasis in social welfare training. The rapidly changing social and economic situation of our times requires constant re-evaluation of social work methodologies. Those who train may need to be re-trained to meet the new demands of the 1970s. The new role of students and consumers of social welfare services in formulating education policies and developing curriculum content calls for recognition. We need to prepare and educate social welfare personnel to be more and more involved in policymaking and social planning for development. We need to stimulate the more positive contribution which schools of social work could make to social research in relation to the needs of national development.

---

[2] United Nations, "Report on an Evaluation of the Family Planning Programme of the Government of Pakistan." Prepared for the Government of Pakistan by a Joint United Nations-World Health Organization Advisory Mission (ST/SOA/SER.R/9, April 7, 1969), p. 130.

In the developmental perspective, social welfare personnel at all levels are called upon to work in an intersectoral context. Social welfare training must be directed toward a stronger emphasis on teamwork and integration with all other activities affecting development. In 1968 the first United Nations Conference of Ministers Responsible for Social Welfare acknowledged the "need for social welfare personnel to become acquainted, through appropriate training, with related areas of practice, to learn to work in partnership with the personnel from other disciplines and to be able to integrate social welfare concerns, processes, and resources with those of other sectors contributing to development. Actually, study arrangement may be advanced in favour not only of the integration of training programmes in social welfare and in related fields, which are now kept quite separate in most routines, but even of a known basic training leading to the ability to perform a variety of tasks through supplementary specialized training or supervised work experience."[3]

It is abundantly clear that, as social work educators and social workers, we have a tremendous task ahead of us. We must deal with the demands and challenges of the 1970s and become completely attuned to issues and problems of universal concern. Our involvement with the totality of man demands from us urgent attention to the problems surrounding and affecting mankind. The preoccupation of social welfare personnel with the changes that are taking place in the social system and its institutions and the emphasis now being given to implementation of policies that promote the development of large numbers of people have made social workers grant mounting importance to societal needs as well as to the needs of the individual. Social work has a unique contribution to make to the problems of concern to this Conference and social work educators have a most challenging role to play as they prepare a new generation and perhaps a new type of social welfare personnel to meet the demands of this decade.

---

[3] United Nations, *Proceedings of the International Conference of Ministers Responsible for Social Welfare*, ST/SOA/89 (1969), page 77.

Perspectives on National Approaches: Government and the People

ANTONIO ORDOÑEZ-PLAJA, M.D.

Throughout his history, man has spent much time and energy in "solving" problems. William F. Pounds defines a "problem" as the difference between an existing situation and a desired one. Since the beginning of the scientific era, it has been an established truth that the fundamental need in problem-solving is an adequate "knowledge" of the problem itself in order to formulate it clearly. Once this has been achieved, the solution or the possible alternatives may be worked out with relative ease.

Knowledge of the population problem, especially in reference to its repercussions in the family and society, is reflected on the political level as a principal motivating force in decision-making, tending to modify an existing situation. The success of family planning programs depends, how ever, on the joint decisions of government and citizens. Disparity between them may be observed in countries whose governments favor population growth but whose citizens have decided on limiting or spacing births and use varying methods toward these ends, or in countries with governments in favor of some sort of action to reduce population growth and whose citizens, at least the majority, have little conscience or comprehension of the problem created by irresponsible profligacy. In some cases, however, agreement can be found between a government conscious of the limitations upon development and well-being caused by exaggerated population growth and a populace, or a good part of it, sufficiently responsible to

Antonio Ordoñez-Plaja, M.D., is former Minister of Public Health, Colombia.

know or try to understand that their number of offspring has a very close relation to the amount of care, attention, and education they can give each child in preparing him to face contemporary problems.

The government knows, through technicians in its service, the socio-economic effects of accelerated population growth upon the progress and well-being of its citizens. It also receives information as to what the felt need of the populace is in the planning of its families: *directly,* through the communication media or from individual organizations, scientific or others; and *indirectly,* from such indicators as abortion rates, infanticides, suicides of parents of numerous families, etc., which augment alarmingly in countries with population explosion.

It is possible that the need for reducing fertility is not felt by some population groups. It is then the task of conscientious parties to awaken these people, to make the community conscious both of its problem and of the possibility for change.

ROAD TO DECISION-MAKING

It is the interchange of concepts between the governors and the governed—a product of the knowledge of the problem and its repercussions—which permits decisions. The process leading to decision-making opens important perspectives as to the efforts of social workers to collaborate on governmental population policies in such a way as to avoid conflicts. On the governmental level, decision-making must be preceded by enough ample and objective information in order to allow problem-solving in a given situation. So, the process appears as the result of interaction between the government, which understands the macro-economic situation, and the family, which feels particular needs.

Neither the governmental decision nor the needs felt by the populace are enough by themselves. Besides this, it is necessary to place information and means in the hands of the families in order to give them a choice (in other words, the possibility of choosing among various alternatives). Therein is seen the great importance of the role of persons or responsible groups who execute programs. They must possess modern techniques and an all-encompassing knowledge of the problem, as well as a philosophical basis which enables them to adjust their actions to the diverse cultural mores that change with locale and time.

In summary, to deal with the population problem efficiently, common accord as to basic premises is indispensable among the varying sectors of government. Similarly, it is necessary that maximum understanding of official policies be achieved by the personnel who must carry these policies out, including the social worker. Finally, though of equal importance, there must be harmony among what the government programs want, what its agents carry out, and what the majority of the population desires.

If these points are not achieved, the results will be fatally negative; for example, families that have not only felt the need to plan their families but also the imperative urgency of doing so faced with a lack of alternatives will turn to measures dangerous to their health and to the stability of their homes. If technicians, among them the social worker, act other than in accord with the concepts fixed by the authorities, they will create a dichotomy between what is offered in words and what is given in fact, with the resulting discredit to the system.

LEVELS OF COMMUNICATION

The fantastic proliferation of publications referring to the theme of birth-control—a veritable bibliographic explosion—is of debatable value. There has been no evaluation of the results of these publications, but, as an example, anyone can note the frequent confusion existing among the terms population control, birth control, and family planning. In the same sense, in newspapers and periodicals which express an emphatic and active policy in regard to family planning it can be frequently observed that alarmist headlines and articles of little scientific basis—and which only produce panic and confusion—are published.

At this meeting what we want to deal with, ultimately, is a communication problem at all levels in social work. In the first place, it is necessary to agree upon what professors of social work should communicate to their students; and in the second place, we must ponder how the social worker can best communicate with the populace.

We must accept the fact that our past means of communication have not proved very effective. It is vital to insist on this last point, relating it with the bibliographic explosion I have mentioned, because we frequently forget that all communication, by definition, has to be in two directions. To speak and not to listen is not communication. It matters not what level of scientific and moral authority the expositor possesses, the epoch of *magister dixit* belongs, fortunately, to the past. Contemporary man, and especially the new generation, can only be motivated through participation, and the first stage of that participation is through communication by dialogue.

CLARIFICATION OF THE PROBLEM

Schools of social work have acquired a conscience—albeit somewhat late in relation to the other medico-social professions—of the importance this profession has in the development of population programs. This fact makes educational leaders even more responsible for designing a corresponding curriculum, and they have the privileged position of being able to take advantage of the experience of sister schools of study by avoiding their errors and studying their successes.

A series of observations which may contribute to a better expression and enunciation of the problem under discussion may now be formulated:

1. If we accept the definition of population policy given at the Caracas meeting,[1] we must establish what quantity and quality of information the social worker should receive.

2. We must obtain the goal of the student's acquisition of minimal basic information in regard to everything related to the alternatives, possibilities, and consequences of family planning. This should be an added skill within his customary activities.

The social worker, like any person trying to solve the demographic explosion, may be tempted, in his drive for efficiency, to offer more than can be technically guaranteed. Technical failures or complications cause distrust among the populace using the methods recommended, without warning of possible risks, and this distrust may lead to the discrediting of the family planning program as a whole. It also may result in a lack of confidence in social workers in particular.

3. It would be of value to ask ourselves if, in the instruction we give the social worker in social anthropology and social psychology, we are placing enough emphasis on the fact that—besides the general concepts of these disciplines—it must be constantly borne in mind that each sub-group has unique characteristics which must be known and understood before action may be taken.

So we return to the theme of communication in the profoundest sense of the word. We all have the tendency of wanting to resolve other people's

[1] "Population Policies in Relation to Development in Latin America," Final Report of Conference held September 11-16, 1967, in Caracas, Venezuela (mimeographed). By population policy is meant a coherent set of decisions making for a rational strategy, adopted by the public sector in accordance with the needs and desires of families and of the community, for the purpose of influencing directly the probable size and age make-up of the population, the size of the family, and the regional and rural-urban distribution of the people, in order to facilitate the achievement of the aims of development. This policy should take into consideration and evaluate the effects on these variables of changes in the social processes, especially education, housing, health, and employment.

problems through the coloring of our own beliefs and sentiments—that is, we act in an egocentric and paternal manner—but we always discover that no one can delineate the happiness of others.

The fundamental objective of all professionals working with a community must be, on the contrary, to help members of that community leave behind a situation of dependency by identifying the situations that can limit their capacities for progress. We must stimulate their potentials for autodetermination and their rational decision-making powers. We must weed out their fatalism, urging them toward a higher estimation of their own worth and of the consequences of their own actions upon their families and communities, and upon the progress of their nation.

Leadership Perspectives: Governmental and Voluntary

ALAN F. GUTTMACHER

"Am I my brother's keeper?" was first addressed to God by Cain in answer to Jehovah's query, "Where is Abel thy brother?" In the intervening centuries, the concept of man's responsibility for his fellow man has grown in breadth and scope. No doubt this sense of responsibility spread first from the nuclear to the extended family, then to the tribe, and later to the nation. In this day of shrinking distances and satellite communication the sense of responsibility for one's fellow man circles the globe. Proof is found in the large amounts of money furnished by the United States Agency for International Development, the Swedish International Development Authority, the British Ministry of Overseas Development, and similar organizations attempting to better the lot of people in the less developed nations.

The concept of a tithe goes back to the Biblical injunction in Deuteronomy. At that time it had the dual purpose of supporting the priesthood and giving succor to "the sojourner and the fatherless, and widow." Originally it was offered in the form of food; later, in more durable possessions such as money or land. The tithe was not purely Hebraic in its expression; in antiquity it was almost universal—Greece, Rome, Babylon, China, and Egypt employed it. In it the germ of the welfare concept first found expression.

From my studies, I gain the impression that teaching methods to control conception for the benefit of the poor did not come into being until

---

Alan F. Guttmacher, M.D., is president of the Planned Parenthood Federation of America, Inc.

the nineteenth century. This does not mean that contraception was unknown earlier. However, contraception, except for *coitus interruptus,* was largely confined to the gentry and then mainly for their extramarital activities. The socialization or democratization of birth control is a relatively recent socio-medical phenomenon: What once existed almost exclusively for the upper classes slowly became a reality for the masses. Medical discussion of the means of birth control is very old, but the stress on the social and economic desirability of birth control is as largely a nineteenth-century characteristic as stress upon the necessity of population control is largely a twentieth-century characteristic. Previous to the nineteenth century the adages "Children are poor men's riches" and "The rich get richer and the poor get children" were taken as gospel, unchallenged as immutable laws of God.

HISTORICAL DEVELOPMENT OF BIRTH CONTROL

The first public challenge to the upper class monopoly of conception control was Francis Place, born in 1771, the father of 15, and an English working man. Between 1823 and 1827, Place and his co-workers—among them, 17-year-old John Stuart Mill—distributed thousands of single-page, printed contraceptive handbills throughout London and the textile areas of the Midlands. His opposition called them "diabolical handbills." The method of birth control primarily advocated was the pre-coital intravaginal insertion of a sponge about the size of a small apple. This technique had been advocated in 1797 by Place's friend, the philosopher-jurist, Jeremy Bentham, to reduce the poor rates, the English eighteenth-century form of a welfare tax. Bentham, unlike Place, took no steps to popularize his idea.

Place stressed the economic benefits the poor could derive from smaller families achieved through birth control. Health benefits to the mother were given secondary importance. Place argued that birth limitation among laborers would create scarcity in the labor market and thereby raise the weekly wage scale. In 1823 children commonly commenced work in the factories at the age of nine which Place deplored because it prematurely terminated their moral and secular learning. He argued that fewer workers would produce adult wages which would make it less necessary to send children to the mills at so tender an age. Place opposed the prescription of "moral restraint"—that is, delayed marriage—proposed by Thomas Malthus 25 years earlier as the means of controlling conception. Place, who had married happily at 17, espoused young marriage as a preventive against vice and prostitution. His handbills started the English birth control movement which was to wax and wane throughout the remainder of the nineteenth and early twentieth centuries, finally culminating in the opening of the first British birth control clinic by Dr. Marie Stopes in 1921.

The American birth control movement had its origins in the pioneer efforts of Robert Dale Owen and Dr. Charles Knowlton. Owen, an intellectual immigrant from England and later a U.S. congressman from Indiana, was strongly influenced by Place. He published a book on birth control, *Moral Physiology,* in New York in 1830. This small book, which went through many editions, advocated *coitus interruptus.* It included case histories to show the good results achieved from adoption of the method. Owen deemed Place's sponge technique physically disagreeable and of uncertain effectiveness, and he claimed that the condom was too inconvenient.

Charles Knowlton, a Dartmouth medical graduate and a New Hampshire practitioner, published *Fruits of Philosophy* two years later. Knowlton's book was more detailed than Owen's. He claimed to have invented the technique he advocated, the post-coital douche. The superiority of the douche rested on the facts that it was cheap, harmless, involved no sacrifices during coitus, and above all placed the control of fertility in the hands of the woman. Knowlton makes a sound case for contraception on medical, social, and economic grounds.

Margaret Sanger Launches a Movement

Owen, Knowlton, and several other Americans were forerunners to Margaret Sanger (1879-1966) who, without doubt, launched the American birth control movement. Her predecessors were advocates of special techniques and for each of them birth control was of secondary interest to their other activities. For Mrs. Sanger, family planning was a consuming cause, a devouring preoccupation, and an almost unconquerable challenge.

Margaret Sanger, the middle child of eleven, was born into a family whose head was a stonemason in a small town in upper New York State. Michael Higgins was an iconoclast and agnostic, with the same indomitable, fearless spirit that became the hallmark of his famous daughter. After graduating as a nurse, marrying, and bearing three children, Margaret began to work on New York's Lower East Side, then peopled by immigrant Jews and Italians. As a visiting nurse, she saw poverty and its concomitant, a plethora of children, at first hand. She found illegal and dangerous abortion the only method of family limitation in practice, as the men refuse to use a condom or *coitus interruptus.* In 1912 a poor Jewish woman, the mother of four, died in Mrs. Sanger's arms after an abortion, and on that day her career was confirmed. She would democratize and socialize contraception so that its practice would become as available to the masses as it already was to the upper social classes.

Mrs. Sanger studied birth control in Europe where she learned the use of the occlusive vaginal diaphragm. In October, 1916, in Brownsville, a slum area of Brooklyn, she opened the first birth control clinic anywhere in the world outside of Holland. The way was not easy, however, for before the center was fully operating, it was raided by the police and Mrs. Sanger was jailed for the first of eight times. In spite of the difficulties, it was through this non-governmental, special voluntary agency that Mrs. Sanger began the world birth control movement.

The Planned Parenthood Federation of America, a lineal descendant of the National Birth Control League started by Margaret Sanger, now operates 525 clinics in 135 cities and serves 350,000 patients a year. This is proof that Mrs. Sanger accomplished her dreams of socializing or democratizing birth control. Further proof is offered by the growth of the International Planned Parenthood Federation, founded by eight nations at Bombay in 1952. Today, it operates with a budget of 10.5 million dollars and has 66 countries as member nations.

CONCEPTION CONTROL AS GOVERNMENT CONCERN

It is obvious that effective birth control cannot be given on a global scale by voluntary agencies alone; it can only be done in partnership with governments. This is clear today, but this clarity is of recent origin. As recently as 1958, Dwight Eisenhower, then President of the United States, publicly stated that providing means for the control of conception was no concern of government but of private philanthropy, a statement which he gallantly retracted several years later. As recently as 1963, in my preface to the reprint edition of Norman Himes' *Medical History of Contraception,* I wrote: "In the United States, the Federal Government virtually takes no notice of contraception."[1] What a change seven years have wrought! The United States Agency for International Development has committed 100 million dollars to help countries that request aid in curtailing population growth. If the Tydings-Scheuer bill passes the U.S. Congress, increasing amounts up to 300 million dollars will be appropriated by the 1975 fiscal year for domestic birth control—service, research, and education.

Involvement of governments in birth control began with India in 1951. Today 75 percent of the governments of the almost two-and-a-half

---

[1] Norman Himes, *Medical History of Contraception* (New York: Gamut Press, 1963), Preface, p. XIII.

billion people living in the developing nations have officially expressed themselves in favor of population control. This does not mean that they are all technically and financially involved as yet. However, a vital program largely financed by government exists in a number of countries, among them: India, Pakistan, Indonesia, South Korea, Thailand, Egypt, Taiwan, and Singapore.

The pattern of family planning varies all over the globe. There are a few countries where there is no family planning activity, either voluntary or governmental. In some, the total movement is in the hands of a volunteer group, as in some of the Latin American republics. Government may not only be uninvolved, but antagonostic. One may also find a partnership between government and the private sector, perhaps most effectively exemplified by South Korea. In a few countries we see the government largely preempting the family planning work previously carried out alone for many years by a private agency.

Why do governments become involved? There are several reasons: economic, social, and medical. Let me give an example.

A few years ago the government of Botswana, earlier known as Bechuanaland, requested the International Planned Parenthood Federation in London to send them consultants to help initiate a family planning program. I was dispatched, along with Dr. James McAllan, IPPF director for East Africa. I was puzzled by the request because Botswana was a large country inhabited by only a half-million people. On our arrival the Minister for Economic Development informed us of their poor financial situation; this was a rural, agrarian, non-industrialized economy with rising unemployment and under-employment. Due to a prolonged drought, cattle raising, previously an important industry, had withered, thereby sending unemployed herdsmen to the towns for scarce jobs. In prospect was a new commercial diamond mine and a copper mine, but because both industries were so highly mechanized only a small proportion of the unemployed would be put to work. It was hoped that curtailment of population growth would improve the immediate economic picture by allowing greater industrialization and that it would eventually aid unemployment by reducing the annual inflow of youths into the labor pool. The Minister of Education informed us that 11,000 children completed the third grade of school each year, but there were places for only 500 to continue further. As the economy improved, Botswana hoped to extend educational facilities, an effort that would be thwarted by sheer numbers unless the birth rate were checked. In addition, we were informed that each year they were losing a significant proportion of their educated young women, such as teaching and nursing students, through the frequency of involuntary pregnancies.

HEALTH PROBLEMS AND HUMAN RIGHTS

The main national health problem which cries out loudest for effective contraception is illegal abortion, a world endemic disease, perhaps second to none in mortality and morbidity. It has been estimated by the World Health Organization that there will be 25 million illegal abortions this year. Careful studies show that in Santiago, Chile, for example, there is one abortion for every two live births, that 45 percent of the emergency admissions to hospitals is for abortion complications, and that 25 percent of the blood used for transfusion in Santiago is given to women ill with abortion complications.

In many developing countries, especially in Africa, such infantile nutritional disorders as kwashiorkor and marasmus (the former from lack of protein and the latter largely from lack of calories) cause extensive death, illness, and mental retardation. I saw many such cases while making pediatric rounds in the great hospitals in Lagos and Ibadan in Nigeria and in Kampala, Uganda. In almost every instance in afflicted infants of 6 to 18 months, one gets the history of acute weaning coincident with the mother's discovery of a new pregnancy. The reasons for acute weaning are unknown because there is no medical evidence that nursing adversely affects the pregnant woman, the child at breast, or the baby *in utero*. I need not remind you that in the African bush there is neither canned nor powdered milk. What is substituted is usually a gruel made from a local root plant which is sweet and satisfying but devoid of protein and low in calories. I have wondered whether the taboo against nursing during pregnancy was not in reality a method of controlling family size. It might either serve to postpone resumption of *coitus postpartum* in an attempt to prevent prompt reimpregnation and consequent premature weaning, or perhaps to increase infant mortality. While polygamy was common in Africa there was an absolute taboo against coitus until an infant was two years old, but now, with polygamy disappearing for economic reasons, the situation has changed. Today coitus is immediately resumed with the only wife.

Finally, some governments have become interested in popularizing birth control as a basic human right for their people. Ability to have babies by choice rather than by chance should not be within the purview of only one segment of the population; it must be a privilege shared by all. The plight of the unwanted and rejected child leading to roaming bands of homeless boys and child prostitutes on the streets of Addis Ababa, Ethiopia, and nurseries and orphanages filled with abandoned babies in Seoul, Korea, have underscored the necessity for effective birth control on a global basis. Even in relatively sophisticated America, a study by Bumpass and Westoff of Princeton University shows that three-quarters of a million babies born in the United States each year are not wanted at the time of their conception.

TASKS FOR THE FUTURE

For the foreseeable future the task of conception control is so immense that there is ample room for both governments and private voluntary agencies to operate at full capacity. The prescription and administration of conception control techniques must eventually become an integrated element in governmental preventive health care. However, educational activities to motivate people to avail themselves of such services may well become an indefinite partnership task between government and voluntary groups.

Before concluding, I should like to stress two points. First, there are immense cultural differences in the acceptability to peoples of various techniques of conception conrol. Therefore, one must be wholly tolerant of what one nation accepts and another rejects. I need not remind you that there are basically four methods to control conception: celibacy in the form of late marriage or failure to marry, contraception, abortion, and sterilization. One or all may have pertinent application to this or that nation. The more of the four employed, the greater the likelihood of achieving the results desired. There is no question that the most effective method of conception control to date is safe, legal abortion on demand, but there are as yet few nations culturally prepared to make use of it. The second point I should like to stress is the acute need for better birth control techniques, techniques requiring less effort by the user and wholly free of undesirable side effects. The latter is particularly important today in view of the unjustified adverse publicity given the pill. We certainly also need systematic methods of birth control which can be used by the male. Improvements in birth control require immense research efforts and liberal government funding.

It is necessary to view the uncontrolled proliferation of mankind as a serious epidemic, an epidemic so serious that it merits total involvement by the whole world for its control. Only when this view becomes universal will mankind be protected against its own consuming fecundity. The question is, will such dedication come soon enough to forestall catastrophe?

Social Attitudes Toward Population Policies in Less Developed Societies

SELO SOEMARDJAN

Almost every country in the world which has emerged from the dark valleys of illiteracy in the past two decades is interested in economic development. In this respect the world observes a clear distinction between the economically advanced and economically less developed countries. The difference, however, is not only in the degree of economic progress but also is rooted in the social systems and cultures of the many societies to be found in the world.

In most of the advanced countries, social institutions, social attitudes, political organizations, and cultural priorities have developed to support the growth of the national economies. In other words, economic considerations play a leading role in the overall development of the society involved and consequently are accepted as guiding principles in other sectors of life.

The situation in less developed countries is different. They are less developed in their economy because in the past they had other than economic goals to guide their development. Whatever sector of life enjoys the cultural focus of a society has a determining influence on the development of all other sectors of life of the people. If at some point in the history of a society that cultural focus shifts to the economic sector, a revolutionary change has to take place in all the non-economic sectors to make social institutions consistent with the new and dominating economic goals. This revolution at present is going on in each of the less developed countries. This paper is concerned with that revolution, par-

Selo Soemardjan is dean of the Faculty of Social Sciences, University of Indonesia, Djakarta, Indonesia.

ticularly where it affects social attitudes toward population policies within the context of economic development programs.

POPULATION POLICIES

Economic development in less developed countries is essentially aimed at improving the material conditions of a society; it is quantitatively measured by the increase of per capita income in that society. Looked at from this angle, economic development is to develop a faster growth of material and financial factors than the growth of the population at large. The faster the growth of the former and the slower the growth of the latter, the more success economic development is likely to achieve.

In order to gain success, however, economic development programs cannot afford to operate only on the material and financial side of the economy but should also seriously engage in solving population problems as being related to the goals of such programs. Planning the material and financial parts of economic development can follow with high probability of success the universally applicable rules of economics, which make use of quantitative measurements and calculations with or without the help of ingenious computers.

Planning the population side—without even mentioning the social side—of the program, on the other hand, involves working with human material, which does not allow the mere quantification of its size and number, but requires the consideration of qualitative faculties in societies and human individuals as well. Because cultural and psychological conditions vary from one society to the other, a wise planner will allow enough weight to idiosyncratic social, cultural, and psychological factors, just as he does to other factors ruled by general principles of sociology, cultural anthropology, and social psychology.

Three principal problem areas stand out for population planners: urbanization, uneven distribution of population, and excessively rapid population growth. The first two problem areas will be discussed only briefly in this paper to serve as a comparison for the problems of population growth and related policies.

URBANIZATION AND MIGRATION

Urbanization, the influx of people from rural areas into towns and cities, becomes a problem only if living facilities in the urban areas do not suffice to meet the need of the increasing population. In most cities urbanization does constitute a problem, but even so, there is hardly any government which makes deliberate efforts to prevent or to stop or even to discourage the transfer of people from rural areas into the city. Most governments and other responsible organizations regard urbanization as a social phenomenon with principally social problems; as a consequence, policies to cope with such problems are much more social than economic in nature. The most important question is how to make living conditions in the city better than they already are. In this endeavor the government needs the actual support of the people, who are expected to observe the norms and values in city life. But almost nothing in the way of norms and values affects the individual directly. Very rarely is an individual required to make a decision by himself on that basis for his own benefit and that of his community. City rules and regulations are for the good of the whole community, and only through the community can their benefit be enjoyed by the individual.

In the case of uneven population distribution, the policies of a government follow a different process. In order to lessen population pressures in an over-populated area, people are induced or persuaded to obtain a better living in other less densely populated areas. Thus, the process proceeds through personal welfare to reach improvement of living conditions for the community. Decisions to participate in migration programs have to be taken by the individuals themselves without or only with very little pressure from the community. In fact, many communities in less developed areas, for reasons of social solidarity and communal affection, are far from being helpful in individual decision-making for out-migration. To obtain success in migration programs aimed at more even population distribution, the government and its agencies have to overcome many social and cultural obstacles which are of no significance and in many cases are not even relevant to the problems of urbanization. Binding family relationships, responsibility for the care and maintenance of ancestors' graves, the fear of leaving the psychological security of tradition for another and unknown social system, the shame at being accused of disloyalty to the community, are but a few social and cultural barriers standing in the way of a migration program. A well-planned information system or a well-directed education system aimed at changing unfavorable social attitudes and belief systems are prerequisites for the successful implementation of the program.

Whatever the barriers, there is in general no disagreement as to the ultimate goals of organized migration, which is the economic well-being of both leavers and stayers. The social and cultural hurdles hamper only the decision to move, and they are in no way matters of principle. Information and education do not have to solve matters of principle, they have only to reinforce the individual's will to break away from his old environments to start a new and better life in another place.

PROBLEMS OF BIRTH CONTROL

The problems of brith control are much more complicated. In less developed countries where people's attitudes and belief systems are not primarily imbued by economic considerations, there can be strong disagreement between different groups on the immediate goals of birth control. The problems also cover a very sensitive subject—sex—and consequently they cannot be discussed or sometimes even mentioned in public without touching moral and emotional feelings. In many instances one should be very careful about even mentioning the subject, because it may evoke resistance stemming from fanatic and orthodox religious beliefs or from traditional ways of thinking. The numerous alternative names for the same program—birth control, population control, family planning, planned parenthood, and the like—are indicative of the many sensitive spots which have to be avoided to get the program socially accepted.

Pessimists on the subject of birth control are likely to give up before starting to implement the program on the grounds of the complexity and multiplicity of problems to be solved. Those with more confidence in the program, however, may find ways and means of solving the problems, if only at the cost of careful planning and more careful execution, strengthened with indestructible patience. The best strategy to adopt in getting a birth control program accepted by the people is to change unfavorable attitudes and belief systems so as to make them consistent with the program. This is not an easy task, because it involves the discarding of well-established patterns of behavior and the acceptance of new and unknown ones. With proper knowledge and understanding of the people's real needs and feelings, however, the task can be sucessfully accomplished.

Role of Government

Before a birth control program gets organized, it is essential that the government of a country accepts the idea that restriction of the number of births will finally be of significant benefit to the people. It is widely known that in less developed countries people largely depend on the government to have new programs initiated. As a consequence, birth control programs are doomed to die before birth if the government is not convinced of their merits for the people. There are many government leaders who think of the strength of a country in terms of the size of its population. The larger the population, the greater the manpower for productive purposes and the more soldiers that can be recruited against foreign enemies. This concept is indeed valid in countries with a low level of technology, but in modern societies it is not the quantity of men that counts; it is the quality.

Political leaders in all countries are intelligent persons, at least they are intelligent enough to understand that rapid population increase in slowly developing economies is ultimately doomed to end up in a process of impoverishment. But politics is a game of interests, either of a group or of their leader, and there is very little economic or human sympathy that enters into it.

In the early 1960s, when Indonesia was engaged in building a great nation, birth control was strongly discouraged as it was considered detrimental to the national goals. It needed a dramatic change of government together with a shift in the national development focus from the political to the economic sector, and from emotional to rational ways of reasoning, to change the government's attitude to favor birth control. The wise policy of the new government was to proceed slowly and cautiously in its efforts to introduce the new value judgment of birth control to the population. Too fast a process might hurt unadjusted feelings, and once that occurred, it would be extremely hard to win people's opinions for the good cause.

The building of a favorable attitude toward birth control is undoubtedly the most fundamental prerequisite for its further programming. As long as there is no consensus on the matter within all government circles, there is little hope of much success in communicating the idea to the people. Again, the principal basis for the formation of an attitude in government circles is interest-oriented politics. In a multi-party political system such as the Indonesian one, there are naturally many kinds of conflicting interests, each trying to fight its way to a dominating position. A complete consensus on a specific issue is seldom achieved, such as on the issue of birth control.

In many less developed and usually still tradition-oriented societies, however, there is an effective instrument to bring conflicting attitudes to merge into one position, even if the underlying interests remain unaltered. This instrument is the general loyalty to the traditional or charismatic leader. Stronger than all democratic political rules and procedures, which are, in fact, of alien origin to the indigenous population, are the traditional norms and values, particularly those pertaining to the leader-follower relationships. Fortunate, therefore, are the societies blessed with recognized traditional or charismatic leaders with an enlightened and realistic eye for the general welfare of the people. Political democracy does not work well in a less developed country if it is devoid of this kind of leadership. In such a vacuum of leadership, however, power and prestige of the government over the population is bound to fail in backing up its authority, particularly in cases of controversial issues such as birth control.

Creating a Climate of Acceptance

But supposing that a favorable established opinion has been established in the government on birth control, what is the next step in getting it accepted by the population? The very first action for the government to take is to realize that it has to work in a vacuum of knowledge about the subject. Another thing to be realized is that birth control can never be made compulsory for the people. This warning cannot be overemphasized, especially for countries where government power is so dominant that officials think that everything can be organized by decree.

An intensive and widespread information campaign has to be carried out to fill the vacuum with knowledge about birth control in all its aspects. The principal goal at this stage is how to get the message through to the audience. Mass communication media and all available modern techniques of information distribution can be applied only in population sectors where literacy and the habit of reading, listening, and watching mass media of communication has become institutionalized. In other illiterate groups of the population, information has to be channeled through recognized headmen of village communities, tribes, and clans in order to lend it the authority of officialness.

The subsequent step to take is to wait, observe, and analyze the various reactions from different groups in the population. Now the essential objective is how to get the message accepted by the public. It is essential that not only verbal reactions are analyzed; it is more important to discover the underlying social, cultural, or perhaps political reasons for unspoken or unformulated attitudes.

Nature of Unfavorable Reactions

A large part of the initial unfavorable reactions may be summarized into three problems. The first one asks: Is sex information, which is the principal part of birth control, a private or a public affair? Sex in most communities is definitely a private subject which should not be mentioned, let alone discussed in public. Sex has such a high value of privacy between a particular man and a particular woman that even referring to it in the intimacy of the family will arouse strong feelings of shame. Sexual relations carried out in deviation of moral norms are in most cases considered a sin or a crime. To give information on the subject of birth control one should therefore give it either to individuals, preferably of the same sex as the informer, or, if this method takes too much time and effort, to a small group of people of similar sex. To induce a higher degree of acceptance by the audience it is preferable that the informer be a man or woman of an age beyond the summit of sexual drive.

The second problem derives from the question: Is reproduction a human act or is it an act of nature? By human act is meant an act subject to human will and human interference according to man-made norms and values. Nature, on the other hand, includes all forces in the physical world which operate beyond the powers of man. The argument here is that if reproduction is a human act, than it is legitimate and feasible for man to control it, but if it is an act of nature man has no choice but to accept it.

This line of thinking, as most cultural anthropologists know, is most common among societies with a low level of technology and very little knowledge of science. Confronted with the powerful forces of nature and unable to understand them, primitive man has no other choice than to surrender to nature. Interference with the mysterious forces of nature would, primitive man believes, only end up in self-destruction. Only by educating him about man's faculties to defend himself against the destructive forces of nature and how to use these faculties for his own benefit can primitive man be made to understand that in the process of birth control the essential point is to create man's will either by restraining his own actions or by the use of force of nature itself to prevent the natural process of reproduction from beginning. Once that process has started to take place there is very little man can do to interfere, at least at primitive man's low level of technology.

The third generation problem is of a higher order: Is reproduction an act of man, or is it predestined by God? This runs parallel to the second problem, but here religious beliefs and man's absolute submission to God play an important part. If human reproduction is God's will and predestined by Him, man's interference would constitute a serious rebellion against the Almighty.

A religion, however, would not be able to stand the challenges of man's progress in life if it failed in finding an acceptable and effective solution for man's social problems. If a society is determined to solve a real need, or if it has firmly set itself to attain a goal, religion has an instrument to help. This instrument is reinterpretation of religious norms.

If a religious norm is in conflict with the real needs of a society, tensions tend to build up until the situation becomes so unbearable for the people that a satisfactory accommodation, if not a final solution, of the conflict has to be reached at any cost. Neither the real needs nor the religious norm can be changed at will, but reinterpretation of the norm for the benefit of the society is allowed. If there is no way of reinterpretation of a religious norm because of its rigidity or simple clarity, another and more favorable norm should be found to supercede the original. This cultural dynamic applies also to the issue of birth control.

It may be of importance to know that religious reasons in less developed societies tend to rank high on the list of birth control rejections. In a recent survey in Djakarta and rural surroundings, 74 percent of the males and 71 percent of the females who disapprove of birth control have their attitudes based upon religious beliefs.

Response to Cultural Reasons for Rejection

However, irrespective of the underlying cultural reasons for rejection of birth control, one should not neglect the verbal reasons against this issue. These are, in fact, the outgrowth of the cultural reasons and should therefore be properly handled as such. A correct and acceptable response to underlying cultural reasons creates a positive conviction. A similar response to verbal reasons builds up satisfaction.

For many people the term birth control is unacceptable on religious and humanitarian grounds, but the same program under the name of "family planning" or "planned parenthood" is widely accepted and unemotionally used. These names seem to emphasize the wisdom of planning the welfare and happiness of the family rather than emphasizing an intentional interference in the process of conception and birth of human beings.

Large groups of Indonesia's population, particularly those of Islamic religion, have raised strong objections to the economic objectives of birth control. In part, their objections stem from the incapacity of many illiterate and poorly educated people to think of macro-economic and futuristic problems, but the objections also originate from people's preference for more humanistic objectives. It was therefore emphatically announced by the Indonesian government that the main objective of family planning is the improvement of the health and happiness of mothers, children, the family, and the nation. The goal of raising the people's standard of living through measures of birth control is only of secondary importance.

Seventy of the most respected leaders of Islam in Indonesia agree that child spacing is not prohibited by Islam if society or the government decides that it is the best for the family and the nation, but it should be considered as an emergency policy and not as an established rule. The present emergency situation overrules the Prophet's message that Muslims should multiply and spread over the world. Consistent with this opinion is the attitude of such leaders who agree that only information leading to an understanding of the methods of family planning is allowed, but no propaganda to create a firm conviction of the merits of birth control.

Other verbal reasons against birth control are generally less convincing than those which have their source in religion. Another source of the unfavorable attitude toward birth control is a society's ideas about children. Children, so the argument goes, are an investment for old age. They are also a security factor against divorce. It is the duty of a legally married couple to raise a family with children who will continue to bear the family name.

There is undoubtedly no one who disagrees with such arguments, and the most profound protagonist of birth control will never argue that birth control is aimed at childless marriages. Birth control is definitely not against the birth of babies, but it warns against the birth of too many babies by comparison with the rate of economic growth. In one survey, which was held in 1968 in Indonesia, every informant agreed that a family should have children, but nobody agreed on a limitless number of children in a family.

In order to reinforce favorable attitudes toward birth control a government should certainly not restrict itself only to the distribution of information. People will be more convinced and therefore be more strongly induced to practice birth control if actual steps are taken to promote that practice. Strictly rational measures might include the prohibition of marriage under a minimum age, shorter maternity leaves, higher costs of delivery, the supply of electricity for home lighting in cities and villages, and a large supply of inexpensive contraceptives.

In short, the measures to be taken are meant to discourage the conception and delivery of babies, together with a lowering of social values for large families.

BIRTH CONTROL PRACTICE

Accepting the idea of birth control is one thing but practicing its methods is quite another. One may on rational grounds firmly and honestly be convinced of the merits of birth control, but to persuade onself to practice it requires courage and determination to overcome personal psychological barriers. Unlike the obstacles to the acceptance of the idea of birth control, which are generally religious, traditional, or cultural in nature, the difficulties over practice come for a large part from psychological sources.

Here again we find a conflict between two attitudes—acceptance on rational grounds and actual rejection of practice for psychological reasons. To accommodate this conflict many mechanisms of defense—such as no permission from one's spouse, ill health, non-availability of contraceptives, no doctors or other trained medical personnel to give help, and no clear instructions on the matter in religious teachings—are ready for use.

In Islamic societies, birth control practice is legitimate only if approved by both marriage partners, but generally neither of the two is bold enough to start discussing the subject with the other. As a consequence, no explicit approval of either spouse will ever be expressed and no actual practice carried out. In fact, fear of personal inconveniences in sexual relations and shame at having one's most closely guarded part of the body treated by other people (medical personnel) are the last barriers against actual practice, particularly for the women. No formal or national propaganda can be fully effective to help them climb over the barriers. The most influential persuaders in this case are generally intimate friends who have carried out the practice themselves and can speak favorably about their experience.

With regard to the silence in Islamic teachings on the subject of modern contraceptives the mechanism of interpretation can be of effective use. It is said that once the Prophet Mohammed, when asked for advice by a man who was in love with a young slave girl but did not want to raise a child with her, approved that he resort to *azal* (*coitus interruptus*). Today there are highly respected Islamic leaders who advocate that the principle of *azal* includes the use of modern contraceptives as well.

It is remarkable in the survey report from Djakarta how many more women than men maintain definite opinions in favor of birth control, and also how many more women than men express readiness to practice contraceptive techniques. This seems logical, however, because by applying such techniques women can expect personally favorable effects such as fewer pregnancies and subsequent deliveries of babies. Men, on the other hand, have nothing to gain personally from the use of contraceptives.

The survey has also disclosed that there is a strong and positive relationship between formal education and the use of birth control methods. It also reveals the tendency of the formally educated to use more modern methods (pills, injections, IUD) while less educated people prefer the traditional methods (rhythm, sponge, douche, withdrawal).

In analyzing the reluctance people show to apply contraceptive methods the present writer agrees with Klineberg that sexual desire and reproductive drive are two separate drives.[1] In the relations between male and female it is in fact sex which constitutes the primary force, whereas procreation is only a byproduct. On the basis of this opinion one may conclude that contraceptive techniques, though aimed at the prevention of conception, should in no way impair the sexual satisfaction of either male or female. No degree of persuasion to practice birth control methods can really be effective in the absence of assurance that there will be no interference with sexual satisfaction.

---

[1] Otto Klineberg, *Social Psychology* (New York: Holt, 1954).

CONCLUSION

The adverse effect of uncontrolled population increase in the development of national economies and the welfare of families is actually felt in less developed societies. Of all the measures to check excessive population increase, birth control has proved to be the most effective. As sex is one of the most sensitive cultural areas of any society, birth control programs in less developed countries have to overcome many serious religious, social, and cultural barriers before actual take-off. The most serious obstacle against birth control, however, is popular ignorance. Once a society has determined population control to be a strategic subject in its development, however, ingenuity of man and his culture provides the ways and means to move aside every obstacle standing in the way of the society's objective. This conviction breeds optimism regarding the acceptance of birth control programs in less developed societies. The problem remains of how to speed up the elimination of ignorance and how to secure the acceptance of people in putting birth control techniques into actual practice.

PART III :
Background Documents

Systems of Social Work Education: A World-Wide View

KATHERINE A. KENDALL

The Conference on Social Work Education, Population, and Family Planning, convened by the Council on Social Work Education in cooperation with the East-West Center, appropriately calls upon international colleagues for a collaborative effort in finding solutions to the universally recognized problem of overpopulation. The participants, drawn from a variety of disciplines and twenty-eight countries, bring many differences in background and experience to the common purpose. Because they are members of a world community of professionals, however, they also bring to the task considerable shared knowledge as well as certain similarities in goals and values.

The background materials for the Conference have been selected with a view to maximizing the knowledge that is shared by all the participants on the subjects of population dynamics, family planning, and social work education. This paper will present a brief view of social work education around the world. A common understanding of the differences as well as the similarities in patterns and content of education for social work should serve to counteract a natural tendency, in the discussions that will take place on educational recommendations, to see one's own professional preparation as a universal model.

Katherine A. Kendall is director of International Education of the Council on Social Work Education and Secretary-General of the International Association of Schools of Social Work.

ORIGINS OF SOCIAL WORK EDUCATION

Social work as a humanitarian impulse and expression of religious concern is age-old and found in almost all cultures. Social work as a professional discipline, however, had its origins in the personal and religious charity, mutual aid, social reform, and social action movements of the nineteenth century. The "scientific charity" of this period, particularly in Britain and America, sought to improve the conditions of the poor by changing the individual; crusading reformers of the same period sought to improve social and economic conditions by changing the environment. Charity became organized as a service to people, described as a "science based on social principles and observations" requiring "recognition of common principles, the adoption of a common method, self-discipline and training, and cooperation."[1] The reformers, in highlighting social action as service to society, looked to research as a way of shifting attention from the deficiencies of the poor to the insufficiencies in their environment. Both the charity organizers and the reformers were soon committed to the need for special preparation for persons engaged in working for individual or social change as a means of helping the poor.

In 1899 an Institute for Social Work Training, the first full-scale school of social work in the world, was established in Amsterdam. This school offered a two-year course combining study of general sociological knowledge, socio-economic problems, and legislation with supervised practical training in various fields of social work. By 1903, training activities sponsored by the London Charity Organization Society led to the development of a two-year program of theory and practice in a formal School of Sociology. In 1904, a summer school of philanthropic work established by the New York Charity Organization Society was transformed into a full-time one-year problem to become the New York School of Philanthropy, the first school of social work in the United States.

The success of these early efforts led to world-wide development of schools of social work. Boston followed New York in 1904; Chicago, Berlin, and Zürich followed a few years later. The movement spread rapidly within Europe and throughout the United States. By 1920, it had reached Latin America where the first school was launched in Santiago, Chile, and in 1922 social work education was initiated in Asia when a Department of Sociology and Social Work was established in Yenching University, Peiping, China.

In 1950, when the United Nations made its first international survey of training for social work, approximately 300 schools of social work were

---

[1] Katherine A. Kendall, "Social Service," *Encyclopaedia Britannica,* Vol. 20 (1967).

in operation in 42 countries. Of the 300 schools, 204 in 24 countries were at that time associated with the International Association of Schools of Social Work. Now, twenty years later, more than 400 schools in 52 countries are members of the International Association and more than 20 countries have organized their own national association or council of schools of social work. The United Nations estimates that there are probably an additional 100 social work programs of various types, formal and informal, that are not yet affiliated to the IASSW.

Most of the increase since 1950 has occurred in Asia and the Middle East, with the new nations of Africa now entering the field with a growing number of educational programs in social work.

STRUCTURE AND CHARACTERISTICS OF SCHOOLS OF SOCIAL WORK

Schools of social work prepare men and women for social work practice in accordance with the educational traditions, degree of social development, and conceptions of social work in the countries concerned. In many countries, social work is recognized as a professional discipline; in some countries, it is not yet so recognized or it is struggling to achieve professional status. Established both within and outside of universities, schools of social work are organized at varying levels of education: post-graduate, graduate, undergraduate, technical, or secondary. Completion of a program of social work education may lead to a degree, diploma, or certificate or the title of social worker. At the international level, disparate patterns of professional education are not peculiar to the field of social work, but the range of difference, from post-graduate to secondary education, may be greater for social work than for most other disciplines.

Increasingly, manpower planning in all regions of the world deliberately encourages the organization of social work education at different levels on the assumption that there is a rational relationship between stated levels of training and designated functions. For example, a high level of education, usually graduate university study, is seen as essential for social welfare planners, policymakers, administrators, researchers, social work educators, advanced practitioners, etc. A middle level of education, offered within or outside of universities, emerges more and more as basic preparation for social work practice with individuals, groups, and communities. A third level of education or training, pitched somewhere between secondary and university education or, in some countries, at the secondary level or lower, is used to produce auxiliaries, aides, or multi-purpose social welfare personnel for work at "the grass roots."

WORLD-WIDE PATTERNS OF SOCIAL WORK EDUCATION

Schools of social work operating at the level of graduate university education are located in North America and in a growing number of the countries of Asia. These schools offer two-year programs leading to a master's degree. In North America, an increasing number of schools of social work offer advanced programs leading to a doctoral degree. Doctoral programs for social workers are also beginning to emerge in India and Japan. Master's degree education for social work concentrates primarily on professional subjects, as it rests upon four years of undergraduate study which combine general education with a strong emphasis on the social and behavioral sciences.

Undergraduate university education is the basic qualifying route for professional social work in Australasia, much of Asia, and most of Latin America. Undergraduate university programs are also found in the Middle East and in a growing number of countries in Africa. These programs are usually three, four, or five years in duration and combine social work training with general education and study in the social sciences. A degree or diploma is awarded for completion of these programs.

Professional preparation in non-university schools of social work is characteristic of much of the European continent, some countries of Africa, and a few countries of Latin America. Most of the non-university schools require completion of higher secondary education for admission and, thus, operate at the level of undergraduate university education. The programs range in length from two to four years. The shorter programs concentrate on social work theory and practice but also offer some instruction in the social sciences. The longer programs offer greater depth of instruction in the social and behavioral sciences as well as in social work. The qualification awarded may be a diploma, a certificate, or the title of social worker.

Exceptions to the general patterns are found in several countries. The United Kingdom, for example, offers programs of social work education both within and outside of universities and at levels of education ranging from post-secondary to post-graduate.

Too little is known to make safe generalizations about the programs, usually organized at the secondary level, that prepare village-level workers, auxiliaries, and technicians. Such programs, which may run from six months to one or two years in duration, have been more widely developed in Africa and Asia than in other parts of the world.

Two new movements, with possible international consequences, are discernible in widely separated parts of the world. In North America, where professional social work education has long been organized at the graduate level, many programs now exist at the levels of bachelor's degree and community college education to prepare workers for non-professional social welfare functions. A movement to organize a good part of basic professional preparation at the undergraduate level in order to increase the supply of social workers is also gathering strength. At the same time, there is a vigorous movement in certain parts of Europe, Asia, and Latin America to establish advanced programs at the graduate level and to push basic training to a higher rung on the educational ladder in order to improve the quality of social work education. Whether the two movements will converge and where they will lead social work education in the years ahead cannot yet be predicted.

Future patterns of social work education are also affected by a changing sex ratio. Traditionally a woman's profession, social work has become increasingly attractive and challenging to men who seek careers in social welfare. In many countries of Asia and Africa, where educational opportunities for women remain limited, men already predominate as social work students. In North America, the United Kingdom, the Commonwealth countries, and northern Europe, men and women are in better balance than before in schools of social work and in social welfare employment. In countries influenced by French traditions and throughout South America, women continue to outnumber men by a large margin.

The more that social work expands its functions beyond traditional nurturing and rescue operations and begins to embrace policy formation, planning, and social change, the more congenial it becomes as a field of service for men as well as for women.

THE THEORETICAL CONTENT OF SOCIAL WORK EDUCATION

United Nations surveys of training for social work have indicated a large measure of international agreement on the basic body of knowledge and the skills that make up the content of social work education.[2] This seems to be true despite the many differences that exist in the auspices and organizational characteristics of schools of social work.

In general, the theoretical content of social work curricula may be described as embracing: (1) the study of man, his biological, intellectual, and emotional endowment and functioning and the social and cultural factors affecting his development; (2) the study of society, its organiza-

---

[2] There have been four United Nations surveys entitled *Training for Social Work* and the fifth is in process. The first was published in 1950 and the others have followed approximately at five-year intervals. Responsibility for the surveys is lodged in the Social Welfare Section of the U.N. Division for Social Development.

tions and institutions, social problems, social change and development; and (3) the study of social work theory and practice.

The humanities, the social and behavioral sciences contribute much of the knowledge that bears on the social worker's general understanding of man and the political, cultural, social, and economic environment. From allied professions, such as medicine, psychology, law, theology, and education, knowledge of man and society is borrowed and reshaped to the purposes and functions of social work. Increasingly, however, the social work profession itself, through research and analysis of its practice, has developed its own theoretical base. The complexity of the subject matter and depth of instruction in the designated content areas are obviously related to the level at which social work education is offered, the time span, and the resources in faculty, library, etc. available to the specific school.

Frequent reference will undoubtedly be made in this Conference to social work methods or, more precisely, to casework, group work, and community organization. Since teaching of the theory and practice of social work in most schools of social work has consisted and, in many countries, still consists of instruction in these methods, either singly or in combination, a brief and necessarily over-simplified explanation of their meaning and purpose may facilitate discussion. As noted later, however, the changes in this particular area of social work education in some parts of the world are of such significance that similarities between the teaching of social work practice today and that of ten or even five years ago are almost coincidental.

Casework early emerged as a professional method in social work practice. The first formulation stated simply: "Casework is the art of doing different things for and with different people by cooperating with them to achieve at one and the same time their own and society's betterment." The many definitions which followed have clarified and refined the meaning of casework as a complex helping and problem-solving process, but all contain certain essential ingredients involving commitment to the worth of the individual, belief in man's capacity for growth and change, use of scientific knowledge in a meaningful professional relationship and problem-solving endeavor, and effective use of resources within the social environment and strengths within the individual seeking help.

The professional method of group work, like casework, makes use of scientific knowledge and skills in human relations to release capacities for growth and change. Community resources, program activities, and group leadership are used in purposeful ways to help groups achieve particular social ends such as neighborhood development and community action. Group leadership is also used to help individuals find self-realization within and through the group.

Community work or community organization as a professional social work method shares with casework a common ancestry in the charity organization movement, but for many years it lagged behind both casework and group work in the identification of underlying theoretical concepts, processes, and techniques. Progress in this direction, however, has been rapid in recent years. At one time seen largely as a process of adjustment between community resources and community welfare needs, community organization has begun to emerge as a means of helping the community as a social system to engage in a systematic process of planned change toward community improvement.

New circumstances and opportunities are beginning to exert a profound influence on these traditional conceptions of social work and professional social work practice. The social aspirations and mass population needs so abundantly evident in Asia, Africa, and Latin America coupled with a pressing concern in the West with the continued existence of stubborn social problems call for an expanded social work role in both old and new societies.

To Western experience the countries of Asia, Africa, and Latin America have added their own evolving contribution of new ways to raise levels of living and improve the quality of life, particularly for rural populations. Indigenous solutions, such as community development, provide fresh methodological approaches which could well be emulated by those countries of the West that are still mired in the unsolved problems of mass poverty.

New targets for social work in many countries now include greater emphasis on the prevention of social problems, creation of equal opportunity for all citizens, mobilization of disadvantaged groups to effect change through their own efforts, the re-structuring of environmental forces and institutions, implementation of planned social change, and active professional involvement with large population groups. In these contexts, the social worker is seen as as agent of social change and a key contributor to social development. His professional methodology may employ a range of interventive, developmental, action-oriented, and advocacy techniques that often build upon but frequently extend far beyond the characteristic approaches of casework, group work, and community organization. In addition, social policy formulation, social welfare administration, social planning, and social work research increasingly come to the fore as recognized methods of professional social work practice taught by some, if not all, schools of social work.

FIELD INSTRUCTION

Field practice has frequently been described as the core of professional education for social work. The assumption that students can and should carry responsibility for client service from an early point in their professional education may reflect the agency-centered beginnings of social work education. Early programs had the intensely practical purpose of preparing personnel for specific agency tasks. Supervised field work was the pivot around which everything else evolved; it still remains an indispensable element in the education of a social worker.

In all countries field instruction serves the purpose of helping the student put knowledge to use in direct work with individuals, families, groups, and collectivities. Although increased attention is now being given to practice in policy formation, planning, administration, and research, the professional methods of casework, group work, and community work characteristically have been emphasized in field instruction. Educational supervision by a qualified practitioner-teacher has generally been regarded as essential to the success of field practice. Professional self-discipline and objectivity have been cited as key educational purposes to be achieved. As noted below, however, much of what has been regarded as traditional in field instruction has been supplemented, if not replaced, in some countries, by approaches that emphasize more independent learning, group consultation and supervision, social action, multi-disciplinary collaboration, etc. While the agency and practice patterns of the West continue discernible in much of what is described around the world as social work, indigenous patterns have definitely begun to take shape in the developing countries, reflecting maturing national goals and evolving systems of social development.

The many changes occurring throughout all of social work education have left their mark on field instruction. The concept of the established agency as the only possible locale for instruction of students has been enlarged in many countries to admit non-traditional services. In the United States, for example, such services include community action programs, tenants' associations, welfare rights groups, labor unions, civil rights organizations and offices of elected government officials. Increased emphasis has also been placed upon practice in the urban ghettos, neighborhood multi-service centers, urban renewal and public housing programs, and public school demonstration projects. Service centers attached to schools of social work—an old idea in Latin America—have emerged as a new departure in the United States, with an added dimension, however, through a special emphasis on teaching, demonstration, and research as well as direct service to clients.

Many more examples could be cited from all parts of the world to illustrate the vigor of field instruction in social work education. Enough, perhaps, has been said to suggest that field practice is of paramount significance in preparing students for increased involvement and service in population and family planning activities.

FUTURE DEVELOPMENTS

It is an expressed purpose of the International Conference on Social Work Education, Population, and Family Planning to make its findings and recommendations widely available to interested social work educators in all parts of the world. It is hoped that schools of social work in the various educational systems will welcome and make expanded use of demographic content in curriculum building and put new emphasis on family planning as a significant area of social work practice. The degree to which this will occur will undoubtedly vary within countries, from country to country, and from region to region, and may depend, to a considerable extent, upon sustained leadership, continuing educational stimulation, and resources in the form of qualified faculty, facilities for field training, and a variety of instructional and library materials.

This Conference can best be seen, therefore, as only the first step in an ongoing process of curriculum change and development. The time is propitious. Regional and national associations of schools of social work, in preparation for the fifteenth International Congress of Schools on Social Work in Manila in the summer of 1970, are projecting educational goals for the 1970s. In many countries a greatly expanded involvement of schools of social work in preparing personnel for a more effective contribution to population policies and family planning programs is certain to emerge as an immediate goal of the most urgent significance to man and society.

Education and Training of Social Workers for Roles and Functions in Family Planning

LYDIA RAPOPORT

INTRODUCTION

This paper is concerned with the need for relevant education and training for social workers to prepare them for significant roles and functions of family planning activities. Social work is new to this area and has developed little experience and expertness, with some rare exceptions. Our task is to explore ways and means by which we may move ahead responsibly through educational development to give the necessary impetus, knowledge, and competence to practitioners at various levels of practice.

BASIC DEFINITIONS OF TERMS AND IMPLICIT ISSUES

Semantic confusion in behavioral and social science areas and in applied fields of practice is not an unusual phenomenon. In the field of family planning and in population dynamics, the need for scientific clarification is crucial if we are to move ahead in a rational manner. Until recently, because of societal taboos, non-respectability, and illegality, various terms have been used which, in essence, are euphemisms. These constraints no

---

Lydia Rapoport is a professor at the School of Social Welfare, University of California at Berkeley. *This article originally was published in the* Journal of Education for Social Work, *Vol. 6, No. 2 (Fall, 1970), pp. 27-38.*

longer operate, however. The persistence of euphemisms and semantic looseness hides basic motivation and intention and therefore obscures what we are about. We need clarification of terms and intentions in order to contribute honestly to the necessary dialogue about issues of social policy in regard to population problems. Clarity is also needed for interprofessional communication in order to move toward a more specific perspective and to communicate with paraprofessionals and the target groups we are trying to serve with health and welfare programs.

Semantically, during this century, there has been a shift in such terms as birth control to contraception, to family planning, and now these are intermingled with problems of population dynamics and population control. Each term has a different intention, purpose, possibility, and limitation, both technical and social. Basically, we refer to three areas of control: *conception control,* which includes all methods of a mechanical, chemical, or surgical nature for preventing conception (e.g., sterilization); *fertility control,* which aims at the prevention of births and includes all measures of conception control plus such measures as the so-called "morning after pill" and abortion; and *population control,* which is directed to the rate of population growth and takes into purview fertility control plus the relation between fertility and mortality, migration, and problems of economic and social development, etc.[1]

The term "family planning" is a more recent phrase. One writer states that "it is intended to be so homey, unexplicit, and inoffensive as to find universal acceptance, and this has almost happened."[2] Family planning as a field of endeavor has many basic concepts built into it. One key concept is the regulation of fertility by preventing unwanted pregnancies, by spacing the number of children desired. This gives families mastery over their reproductive functions and enlarges their capacity for choice and self-direction in individual and private family goals. Self-determination, choice, and effectiveness in family planning are important ethical and behavioral considerations. "Every child a wanted child" is the popular slogan. Family planning is also embedded in the health matrix and seeks to make an impact on foetal wastage, prematurity, maternal mortality and morbidity, and child health. It is also rooted in concepts of social and psychological well-being in its emphasis on strengthening the quality and stability of family life; thus, it becomes a

---

[1] Philip Hauser, "On Non-Family Planning Methods of Population Control," unpublished paper presented at the International Conference on Family Planning, Dacca, Pakistan, February, 1969.

[2] Reverend Don C. Shaw, "Barriers to Fertility Control," with Special Reference to Low Income People," *Family Planning-An Option for All People* (Chicago: National Federation of Settlements and Neighborhood Centers, 1969), p. 3.

measure for positive mental health. Family planning objectives include not only conception control but also help with problems of infertility, although this dimension is underplayed in actual practice. Thus, family planning deals with the promotion, postponement, and prevention of conception. The development of programs and services are expressions of the concept of the basic right to access to information and service for all as part of the broad human right to health and well-being with equal protection of rights to self-determination and freedom of choice. In essence then, family planning deals with the vital concern of fertility control via individual and family behavioral acts which will help produce wanted and planned children.

Historically, the family planning movement has been motivated by numerous opinions and purposes from liberating and protecting the social rights of women to advocacy of population control and eugenic selection. Professor Shlakman pointed out that "the attainment of official sanctions for fertility control has probably been facilitated by an unofficial or tacit coalition of diverse interests and the argument marshalled in support of different approaches persuaded different publics. This has left us with a residue of confusion which can hamper effective policy developments."[3] From the policy declarations within the family planning literature she identifies 13 divergent purposes, one of which is to control total population. I concur with her when she cautions against hiding anti-natalist policies under the guise of family planning.

It is highly undesirable, for many cogent reasons, to use the growing movement and practice of family planning as a way of backing into the complex problems of population control. One reason is that family self-determination and population control clash sharply where they intersect. Another reason is in regard to target groups to be served—such as the poor and certain ethnic and racial groups—which tend to be singled out for emphasis. The need to equalize services to enhance family planning opportunities is different from expressed concern about excess fertility in these groups. We are going through a historical period characterized by a great self-consciousness in different class and ethnic groups linked with a growing pride in identity, with affirmation of self-determination and a movement towards the concept and practice of community control and self-help. Some have labelled these trends as aspects of a social revolution. It therefore becomes urgent that professionals in the population field be very clear about purposes and goals as well as means. The

---

[3] Vera Shlakman, "Social Work's Role in Family Planning: Social Policy Issues," *Family Planning—The Role of Social Work,* Florence Haselkorn, ed. *Perspectives in Social Work,* Vol. 11, No. 1 (Garden City, N. Y.: Adelphi University School of Social Work, 1968), pp. 70-71.

charge of genocide has emanated from some segments in the black community; such a charge may have its distorted and self-destructive overtones from one point of view, but it is understandable from the perspective of the insider, the racially oppressed ghetto dweller who has been the recipient of lifelong cumulative discriminatory and oppressive practices. Any propensity to distortion or to group paranoia is reinforced by policy and programs which single out the poor and specific ethnic groups, especially if they are then reinforced by coercive and punitive practices which unfortunately have been known to exist in some public welfare departments and even in our legal system. Social justice becomes a primary issue. Population policy and family planning programs must be beamed at the society as a whole with scrupulous avoidance of practices which might contribute to the politicalization of necessary efforts. Here we might cite Margaret Mead, who stated that "we have to have an ethic on the subject of population control that is worldwide, that includes every one, where class, ethnic and racial difference will not confuse the issue."[4]

The problem of rapid population growth is an increasingly urgent concern. The issues involved need to be dealt with separately, seriously, and honestly as problems in national and social policy and deserve much careful thought, study, and public debate in regard to means and consequences for the whole society. The problems of overpopulation are a high-priority concern for both developing and highly industrialized nations. The United States seems at the brink of moving into such an arena of public policy considerations, stimulated by growing popular concern regarding broader aspects of physical and social ecology and further stimulated by recent presidential pronouncements and legislative activities.

Population experts, demographers, and other social scientists who are fundamentally concerned with population problems tend to see family planning efforts, even if widespread and comprehensive, as nonsignificant means of reducing the population. This is a controversial area. To put forth this position, the demographer and sociologist, Kingsley Davis, is cited at length. According to Davis, the terms *population control* and *population planning* should not be used synonomously with family planning. He defines population control as "deliberate determination of all aspects of human demography, including geographical location and movement, age-sex structure, mortality, fertility and total size."[5] His thesis is

---

[4] Margaret Mead, "The Need for an Ethnic," in *Family Planning and Medical Education, Journal of Medical Education,* Vol. 44, No. 11 (November, 1969), Part II, Chapter 4, p. 32.

[5] Kingsley Davis, "Population Policy: Will Current Programs Succeed?" *Science* (November 10, 1967), pp. 730-739.

that family planning does not provide for fertility control but provides only for a reduction of fertility. The assumption has been that family planning will lessen population growth. However, millions of individual private reproductive decisions do not automatically control population for society's benefit. Family planning can therefore reduce fertility only by the margin that unwanted births constitute all births. Dr. Franklin Robbins states that family planning is but one facet of population control and might be considered to relate to it much in the same way the private practice of medicine relates to public health.[6] Another demographer, Philip Hauser, asserts that "it is doubtful that family planning programs, as conducted at present, can significantly reduce population growth rates during, at least, the remainder of this century."[7]

Direct rather than oblique approach to overpopulation requires fundamental social and economic changes in society which may be painful and politically or morally unacceptable. The changes would have to be basic enough to affect powerfully reproductive motivation and behavior. Davis, in the article previously cited, enumerates many of these measures, some of which he himself characterizes as a chamber of horrors. However, there can be positive inducements as well as deterrents and constraints. In a recent paper, Bernard Berelson offers a most lucid and comprehensive statement as to the kinds of proposals and measures that might have to be undertaken and the obstacles likely to be encountered if a serious population control effort were to be instituted as part of social policy.[8] Such measures need to be explored, studied, and debated in the public realm, separately, and unlinked from family planning programs.

A similar unfortunate linkage, related to the above and affecting the profession of social work in particular, has been the linkage of family planning to the efforts to eradicate poverty. To state the issues briefly here: there are proponents who feel that concerted family planning can make real inroads in helping poor families break out of the poverty cycle. Others—mainly economists, sociologists, and even some family planning experts—maintain that problems of poverty have to be fought with other means, mainly economic and social in nature, which are more relevant to problems of poverty in an industrialized society. Just as family planning cannot be offered as an anti-natalist policy, similarly it cannot be

---

6 Franklin Robbins, "Population: A Hopeless Case," in *Family Planning and Medical Education, Journal of Medical Education,* Vol. 44, No. 11 (November, 1969), Part II, pp. 14-19.

7 Hauser, *op. cit.*

8 Bernard Berelson, "Beyond Family Planning," *Studies in Family Planning,* No. 38 (February, 1969). Publication of The Population Council.

offered as an anti-poverty measure, except as a prescription for *individual* families where family planning can contribute to the maintenance of a better balance between family income and family size.

SOME IMPEDIMENTS TO SOCIAL WORK PRACTICE AND CURRICULUM BUILDING IN FAMILY PLANNING

It is a fact that the profession of social work in the United States has not been at the forefront of leadership in regard to furthering the cause of family planning, neither in terms of broader social policy development nor in terms of programmatic development and service delivery. Indeed, this whole human problem area has been seriously neglected by the social work profession. This situation is particularly strange in view of the fact that this profession generally has moved very quickly in response to many challenges for service with various defined population groups and newly emerging social problem areas, and specifically in view of the fact that the goals of family planning are not charged with conflict or dissent for social work. Florence Haselkorn rightly points this out and notes the compatibility of the value base of family planning and social work in regard to the right to opportunity for self-realization and the right of self-determination regarding freedom of choice in decisions affecting one's own fate.[9] Furthermore, there is great compatability between social work and family planning at a level of more instrumental values in regard to enhancing, strengthening, and preserving of family life, which are central concerns to social work.

Several reasons which have contributed to this state of affairs might be identified. One is the lack of a firm tradition in this country, with some exceptions, for the profession to operate at a level of social policy development. Currently we are striving to emphasize this area. A related reason is the often noted function of social work in our society which is designated as residual in contrast to an institutional function. Basically, that means that the profession is largely concerned with problems of social breakdown and with social disorganization, dealing with residual problems caused by social and cultural lags in institutional development.

Social work has not developed a strong role in prevention, both on the level of provision of services as institutionalized for the entire society and on the level of promotion of health and well-being. We have operated

---

[9] Florence Haselkorn, "Value Issues for Social Work in Family Planning: An Introductory Note," in *Family Planning: The Role of Social Work,* F. Haselkorn, ed. *Perspectives in Social Work,* Vol. 11, No. 1 (Garden City, N. Y.: Adelphi University School of Social Work, 1968), p. 8.

largely in the realm of secondary and tertiary levels of prevention (as defined by the field of public health), which means in remedial and rehabilitative efforts. We tend to deal with populations already identified as problematic or "sick" and are less responsive to working with populations potentially indentifiable as "at risk" or healthy populations in need of basic services. In contrast, family planning has a strong preventive perspective and institutional dimension. Therefore, social work, by its tradition, has not grasped the opportunity of making impact there. This becomes even more paradoxical in view of the fact that "family planning has a far reaching potential for preventing and reducing the incidence of many of our most plaguing problems."[10]

Another possible reason for the lack of high social visibility and activity in family planning is due to the fact that family planning is generally conceptualized as a basic health measure and is offered in a spectrum of health and medical services. Although medical social work is an old and respected specialty area of practice, it is a relatively small part of total social work practice. Furthermore, where social work has been in an "ancillary" position (we have often changed the words but not the position)—in this case a paramedical professional—it has rarely been able to exert strong initiative and leadership. For years the enabling and facilitating function and role of social work in so-called secondary settings has been conceptualized. This role suggests the image of smoothing over, filling in gaps, and raising the quality of service on an individualized basis —a not unimportant task. But we have been slow to grasp the potential for social work to lead, develop, and promote institutional and service delivery change.

The overall compatibility of basic values between social work and family planning should not obscure the fact that there are other serious complex value issues which may have contributed to the relative professional passivity of social work in the family planning field. The most obvious issue concerns human sexuality and the changing mores in regard to pre-marital, extra-marital, and adolescent sexuality. Scientific knowledge in regard to the effects of such change on people and on the social fabric is lacking; this forces professional practitioners in all service fields to fall back on their personal beliefs, attitudes, and mores. The whole area of sexuality is still highly charged. Social workers cannot deal comfortably with this subject despite frequent denials to the contrary. The paradox has been pointed out that professional social workers are knowledgeable

---

[10] Florence Haselkorn, "The Responsibilities and Opportunities for Social Work in Family Planning." Unpublished paper delivered at University of North Carolina Seminar (November 21, 1969), p. 2.

and comfortable with psychosexual development knowledge and the unconscious aspects of sexual drives, needs, and even aberrations, but are uncomfortable with conscious sexual behavior, feelings, and practices. To quote Haselkorn again, "One can only speculate why, despite social work's unique access to the most private feelings and experience of people, there is no evidence that it has acquired a body of empirical observation about sexual behavior."[11] It should be noted that other health professionals, including doctors and nurses, unless specially trained and prepared for family planning functions, also have observable difficulties. Much of the literature dealing with family planning bypasses human sexual feelings, needs and responses. Contraceptive behavior is most often dealt with as separate from sexual behavior. Furthermore, much of what passes for sex education for young people is essentially reproductive biology represented in nonhuman imagery. Brewster Smith underlines this observation: "The neutral language in which family planning is discussed scientifically and professionally should not let us forget that we deal here with sex and the marriage bed, around which surely are woven some of the strongest and least rational motives, the most intimate and private relationships and the firmest institutional norms and taboos known to man."[12]

Other value issues that contribute to complexity and uncertainty, in addition to the discomfort with the subject of human sexuality in all its more raw forms, have to do with dilemmas such as the invasion of privacy and the need to safeguard it and individual freedom as opposed to the need for social responsibility and the professional's role in the exercise of social controls. These are technical as well as philosophical issues around reaching-out approaches which can border on the verge of the aggressive; however, they can only be indicated here as areas in need of further clarification.

An examination of the impediments to curriculum development suggests a whole host of other difficult problems that are not only specific to content of family planning. We are in an important period of transition and change, almost in the nature of an upheaval. The growing complexity of social problems has brought a profound sense of urgency for more and better problem-solving efforts in a wider area of social need. We are confronted with many conflicting demands, a re-ordering of priority efforts, and a demand for "relevance" which is defined differently by various sectors of our constituency. There are, therefore, many competing

---

[11] Haselkorn, "Value Issues for Social Work in Family Planning," *op. cit.*, p. 10.

[12] Brewster Smith, "Motivation, Communications, Research and Family Planning," in *Public Health and Population Change, Current Research Issues.* (Pittsburgh, Pa.: University of Pittsburgh Press, 1966), pp. 70-89.

areas for content inclusion. For example, we are continually pushed to the growing edges of practice in social problem areas such as delinquency control, mental retardation, geriatrics, alienated youth, drug abuse, alcoholism, racism, urban decay, and disorganization. We are also pushed towards new methodoligical approaches which are often too readily espoused without requisite testing, selection, and validation. At the same time we are struggling to define the nature of the core curriculum, to determine what is basic for all learners and practioners. If we cannot define our core character we become chameleon like, without a central identity. When the pressures and demands become inordinate, we retreat to a defensive position and aver that we cannot be all things to all men, nor can we spread our resources so thin that there is no hope of being effective in any arena.

The problems of curriculum saturation, the wish to avoid curriculum construction via the additive method, the balance between generic education and specialization of content and its timing, and the commitment philosophically to a holistic approach are certainly not unique to social work education. They are equally troublesome, for example, to medical education.[13] They are inherent in the nature of professional development, in the fact of rapidly expanding areas of knowledge and in ever-widening areas of social responsibility and societal expectations. To keep up with these dynamics, professional education must engage in a constant effort of curriculum design and revision and must build into the learner and practitioner a concept of life-long study for the profession through various mechanisms of self-development and more formalistic continuing education.

Another impediment is the lack of ready visibility of social work roles in family planning. Curriculum changes usually come about through community pressures to develop new programs with a clear social service component or social work role. Although schools of social work tend to see themselves in leadership roles and on the growing edge of practice, in fact, most tend to lag behind the actualities of practice. There simply has not been the demand for highly trained social work manpower in family planning in contrast to other well-defined manpower needs. On the service level in family planning programs run by the traditional medical team, there is often the spoken or unspoken question, "What do we need a social worker for?" This implies that social work has to sell itself by demonstrating its competence and potential contribution.

---

[13] George James, "The Role of the Medical School in Family Planning," in *Family Planning and Medical Education, Journal of Medical Education,* Vol. 44, No. 11 (November, 1969), Part II, Chapter 10, pp. 115-123.

However, where qualified social work manpower has existed, it has been used extremely effectively. We are now beginning to have social work role models in family planning who are utilized in a wide variety of tasks and roles and who clearly do make a significant contribution. Increasingly, work in family planning can become a viable career choice for the professionally trained social worker.

There are pioneering social workers who have been operating in primary family planning settings, in a range of direct and indirect service roles, though not in sizable numbers. They have been able to do this without having any special educational preparation because of the ability of social workers to transfer and build on basic social work knowledge skills. The activities on the direct service level have been in clinical settings such as in Planned Parenthood Clinics, special Maternal and Infant Care projects, obstetrical wards and gynecology clinics, medical teen-age clinics, public health clinics, clinics under the auspices of the Office of Economic Opportunity, and so forth. Direct service functions are connected with screening, intake, counseling, referral to community resources, follow-up and out-reach programs. Other roles, indirect or facilitating, are frequently taken—administrating local programs, executive functions, consultation to other health personnel, health educator roles, community organization roles, staff development and in-service training, and research.

Social workers are already working with various high risk groups—such as unwed mothers, the mentally ill, mentally retarded, child protective services, well baby clinics, etc.—on both preventive and more often, rehabilitative levels. They already have a mandate and responsibility for the care of such patients as part of more traditional practice. This large core of social workers could be more consciously directed to help those clients and others obtain family planning services as part of the overall social services being given.

POTENTIALITIES FOR CURRICULUM BUILDING

An examination of current curriculum offerings in schools of social work indicates lack of substantial content on family planning and population problems.[14] The difficulty lies in opposite approaches to curriculum development: the additive versus the integrative approach.

In order to develop a new specialty area some new knowledge and information must be added or built into existing courses. Adding new

[14] A summary of the current status of education for social workers in family planning is available upon request.

knowledge and information as such is relatively simple, except for the competing areas of interest which all vie for curriculum time and the question as to the appropriate level and timing. More cogent is the issue of the rapid obsolescence and change in knowledge and the need to help the practitioner continue to acquire knowledge as a lifelong quest. In the integrative approach, knowledge, issues, and problem-solving approaches are dealt with in the context of a broad range of social problem areas. There is less opportunity to build cumulative knowledge and to develop specialist sophistication in any one social problem area.

Some chronic and plaguing questions confronting curriculum builders are as follows: What is essential knowledge; from what sources should it be drawn? How should the rapidly changing nature of knowledge and its obsolescence be dealt with? What aspects of knowledge are in the nature of general education and what needs to be selected out for professional uses? Which levels of education should provide for what kinds of knowledge—for example, should knowledge of demography, population dynamics, basic concepts of family organization and family functioning, reproductive biology, and contraceptive technology be part of undergraduate or graduate professional offerings? What if it is not available in the undergraduate curriculum? At what level of specificity or concreteness should knowledge be presented in contrast to the degree of abstraction and conceptualization as a means of generalization and transferability of use?

Haselkorn deals with these issues lucidly, making a strong case for the presentation in professional schools interface concepts with emphasis on linkages in knowledge and technique for transferability in learning. She argues essentially for an integrative approach, while recognizing that certain issues of a value nature, social policy considerations, legal questions and the implications of the rapidly changing nature of contraceptive technology as to physiological, medical, psychological, and service delivery aspects do need special attention and are specific to family planning and population problems. However, the selection of knowledge in the foundation courses in a graduate professional school should be geared towards a special perspective of complexity and problem focus to move the learner to an emphasis on problem-solving. The task in the presentation of knowledge is to sensitize a student to and increase his awareness of an issue and to provide him with basic conceptual tools for analysis. Basic information courses, it can be argued, belong in an undergraduate curriculum.

Given this perspective, the basic sequence on human growth and the social environment should contain content on biological and psychological aspects of sex, reproduction, pregnancy and childbirth, and contraceptive technology. Family structure and evolving roles within the family life cycle and the impact of family size in regard to family functioning should be examined in the context of class and ethnic cultural variables. Sexuality at all developmental stages should be taught in terms of achievement of identity, autonomy, mastery, and capacity for choice and self-direction. Factors in development that lead to maladaptive responses and psychopathology that diminish capacity for choice and mastery need to be identified.

The social policy sequence can easily be re-ordered in its priorities to give central attention to world population issues, population patterns and the reciprocal effects of great social trends such as economic development, attempts to eradicate poverty, industrialization, automation, urbanization, environmental pollution, war, migration, growing ethnic self-determination, the changing role and status of women, entry into the labor market and its effect on family structure and family relationships. The social implications of a national policy for population control should be explored with attention to political and moral issues, anticipation of social consequences and an examination of the social work profession's stance and role in policy formation. Legal constraints against abortion and sterilization can be explored with examination of the effects of changing legislation. Against this kind of backdrop, social welfare programs and health care services with particular attention to maternal and infant care can be examined as to general population served, with particular attention to the needs of special population groups at high risk and with equal attention to preventive as well as remedial services.

All methods employed in problem-solving in social work are relevant to the family planning enterprise. The direct service methods, casework and group work, still receive heavy emphasis in the professional curriculum. They could readily be geared for application in family planning work. Group work approaches are particularly applicable to educational and preventive goals and can be directed to special interest and problem groups such as the ex-mental patient, the mentally retarded, unwed mothers, welfare recipient mothers, etc. Group work techniques can bring greater sensitivity and personalization to the whole enterprise of sex education for youth.

The casework method is essentially geared to the individualization of services. This is a much broader conception than its equation with psychotherapy. Some family planning strategists emphasize that all energies should go into the basic provision of services to that motivated part of the population which is not served at present but would be competent users with ready access to service. Although such a priority should be stressed, it does not negate the fact that for many people effective contraceptive usage involves complex feelings and behavior which they cannot manage unaided and which may need some clarification, support and reinforcement. Indeed, social work has a special commitment to those who are less effective in social functioning. Haselkorn elaborates forcefully on this controversy: "Conventional wisdom tells us that there are some women who are unable to take advantage of opportunity for reasons of limitation in capacity and motivation. It is precisely when motivation and capacity are obstructed by an interplay of intellectual, social and emotional factors that the one-to-one relationship is the social work method of choice. Nor will adequate institutional arrangements, when we ever finally achieve them, eliminate the need on the part of some for mediating help to locate and utilize and persist in the use of family planning. Follow-up of the drop-out cannot easily be handled by community approaches."[15] She sees the purpose of casework as a clarification of life goals for people uncertain of their wishes and plans relating to family size and spacing, and for those who need to clarify their fears and confusions regarding contraceptive usage. On a more complex level, individualized services given by more sophisticated clinicians are also needed for people who have suffered more severe ego damage and whose total approach to living tends to be chaotic and disorganized. Casework may not be able to reverse the process or alter the character structure, but it can help people to use services more effectively when impediments are reduced to a minimum and supports are maximized. It is unfortunate that polarities have been engendered by many, both in social work, family planning, and outside the field, as to where the major thrust of the professional effort needs to be. Frederick Jaffe talks of the environmental view, which is geared to outreach programs and service networks, versus the cultural approach, which locates deficiencies in people and calls for remedial action through counseling and education.[16] The polarity is artificial and reductionist. The uniqueness of social work is precisely its prescription to both views in what I have called a "bifocal point of view." Haselkorn supports this point, stating that the so-called "environmentalist and cultural approaches coalesce in social work's psychosocial approach."[17]

Community development and community organization is growing

---

[15] Haselkorn, "The Responsibilities and Opportunities for Social Work in Family Planning," *op. cit.*

[16] Frederick Jaffe, "Family Planning and Public Policy: Is the 'Culture of Poverty' the New Cop-Out?" Paper presented at the American Sociological Association meeting, San Francisco, California, August 29, 1967.

[17] Haselkorn, *op. cit.*

rapidly as a significant method of intervention by social workers. Strategies for social change—including political action—receive major attention. Community organization on the neighborhood level geared to self-help efforts and the development of local services and programs is another level of intervention. Both these levels of action are relevant for and can be taught as applied to the family planning enterprise.

The so-called facilitating methods such as supervision, consultation, and administration at present get only limited attention in the graduate curriculum. They are generally geared to more experienced students whose early career goals involves roles which make use of these methodologies. Supervision and other methods of teaching and training are of great use for the development of nonprofessional (and professional) personnel. Administration and program development is more often an acquired skill rather than an area for which there has been intellectual and experiential preparation. Consultation is a newer method of problem-solving which has a growing body of theory that can be taught systematically, particularly to the more experienced student. A good part of the work in the family planning field calls for skills in consultation to personnel within the agency and, much more likely, to other community agencies, professionals, and nonprofessionals. Collaboration is also a method of working, generally in an interdisciplinary context, but aside from exhortations, it usually gets scant attention. Family planning clearly requires an interdisciplinary team approach. At the very least there should be content regarding the subcultural value orientation of other professional disciplines and knowledge of and respect for each other's competence and contribution.

The field work practice experience could provide students with almost unlimited opportunities for some aspect of family planning work. Student training could make much greater use of already existing family planning services for work with individuals, groups, and communities and for development of skills in direct patient services and in a whole host of roles previously discussed. In addition, on the direct service level, almost all work in agency settings lends itself to attention to the family planning needs of clientele.

The research sequence provides great opportunity for engaging student interest in the exploration of many unanswered questions in family planning where there is a vital need for knowledge in a relatively new field. The focus of research should be related to social work practice issues and should also take advantage of the kind of access and intimate relationships the social worker has with this clientele group. For example, survey research, such as epidemiological and demographic data collection, does not need the insight and understanding which are unique to the social work profession. Several areas are natural for social work research efforts: (1) program evaluation in regard to the effectiveness of services in achieving program goals and objectives, evaluation of experimental approaches of an out-reach or preventive nature including health education and sex education efforts, assessment of demonstration-type programs geared to new population groups or high risk groups such as teen-agers, evaluation of qualitative aspects of services given by nonprofessionals and the use of differential manpower in general, etc.; (2) follow-up studies of ineffective users, drop-outs, and effective users for understanding of differential variables making for effective usage, and follow-up studies of high risk groups; (3) studies of a qualitative nature to yield insights regarding attitudes and motivation in use of family planning by different population groups, more subtle analysis of the impact of family planning on family well-being, mental and physical health, family life-styles, marital roles and adjustment, and teen-age sexuality and behavior; studies on the effects of pregnancy testing and pregnancy and abortion counseling; studies of failure to regulate fertility among supposedly informed and motivated women in relation to maladaptive or ineffective coping and life styles. The qualitative studies could yield insights which could generate hypotheses for systematic study and testing; they could also yield insights for greater capacity for prediction of behavior and need which could serve as feedback for program design. Many of the areas of inquiry indicated above can be started and carried out by social work students with faculty supervision and by social work practitioners. Some studies fall within the specific competence of social workers; some they can contribute to through interdisciplinary participation; other types of inquiries are more logically investigated by other disciplines.

TRAINING FOR SERVICE ROLES

A bare sketch of the present curriculum areas in graduate schools of social work with potentialities for training for work in family planning by no means is a sufficient indicator for the multiple training needs or possibilities of the field. It leaves many questions unanswered, particularly the problem of training and education for different levels of practice. These can only be touched on briefly here.

Specialist roles in family planning are emerging which require either more concentrated education in graduate school or for which some advanced education and practice is required. Education for specialists should draw from a broader interdisciplinary base. It may have to be fashioned from offerings in advanced programs in schools of social work, schools of public health, and centers for the study of population problems. The roles may be geared to policy development, program design, and implementation, administration, evaluative research, and program and administrative consultation.

The practitioner emerging from a professional school who has acquired the knowledge of family planning objectives, problems, and programs should be able to apply this knowledge in family planning programs and services. He should be equipped to operate with reasonable self-direction and independence at least in the direct service roles applying clinical skills in the individualization of services. He should be alert to the needs of special problem cases and to be able to participate in the development of new services, including education, and information out-reach programs, and be able to develop group approaches to designated populations. He should also be able to help with the training and supervision of volunteer staff and community aides or new career workers as part of their orientation and continuing work.

The worker who has a general education on the college level but is lacking in professional education is called on increasingly to play a very direct role in family planning. He is to be found primarily in the basic public welfare services and in health agencies and other voluntary services. The college-educated but professionally untrained worker has needed a good deal of training through various means of staff development and in-service training for all phases of his work. To make him effective in the role of initiating discussion of family planning services for his clients, sensitive discussion of attitudes and feelings, enhancement of motivation and effective referral and follow-through, he will need a good deal of systematic knowledge in this area that the agency will have to provide. At this point, the agency will need expert outside help in designing content and teaching methods for such staff development programs. The first emphasis may be on training the supervisory and in-house training staff in order to provide a cadre of personnel who can continue to train new staff and to lend active and continuing supervision to sustain such an effort. Useful training materials and experimental teaching approaches to conveying content with opportunity for working through of anxieties and ambivalent attitudes, such as through methods of role playing, are increasingly being available.[18]

The use of social service and health aides who are members of local communities and of the ethnic population to be served—the so-called indigenous worker—is a fast-growing means of providing both necessary manpower and opening up new career opportunities for previously unem-

---

[18] Miriam Manisoff, ed., *Family Planning Training for Social Service* (New York: Planned Parenthood/World Population, 1970).

ployed or under-employed individuals. It has great potential if roles and tasks are clearly defined and specified, and if adequate training and continuing supervision and support suitable to the needs and abilities of this group is provided. Health and social service aides are being used successfully in many types of agencies, including family planning clinics. They often make a significant contribution and are effective by functioning in ways that the professionally trained social worker cannot, mostly because of the problem of social and professional distance from the client group to be served. The aides are used in our-reach programs to specific neighborhoods, in one-by-one case finding, in referral to various community resources, in supportive relationships through the family planning clinic procedures, and, most important, in supportive relationships which help to sustain the follow-through effort. They are also very helpful in follow-up work. They play a central role with ambivalent clients who lack knowledge or are fearful about services and who may have multiple health and social problems as well as personal or family crises which need attention. Without a comprehensive approach, the family planning effort made by these families becomes sporadic or ineffective because of other pressing, unsolved, and overwhelming problems. The aides become a key resource in identifying, mobilizing, and sustaining resources and motivation fortified by the back-up services of other more highly trained or specialized personnel.

Training for social service and health aides is still evolving and is probably of an uneven quality and effectiveness with much trial and error experimentation and not enough synthesis and building on known successful approaches. Often the staff in training and supervisory capacities is not sufficiently schooled in educational techniques and approaches. In this area, as with staff development programs for the college-educated social worker, consultation by social workers competent in educational methods through teaching and supervision is needed to help with design of content and, more important, with training and supervisory formats and methods that can be geared to staff and what is appropriate to their level of educational and cultural background and learning styles.

From the foregoing discussion it can be concluded that education and training for the great variety of roles and tasks in family planning is needed on a broad spectrum of educational levels. Ways and means of developing relevant content in professional schools is one task. Staff development and in-service training methods, including the use of supervision and consultation, are the most obvious and traditional means of reaching our greatest manpower pool—the partially trained and completely untrained workers. The mechanisms of continuing education, either under professional or university auspices, is becoming a more important device for up-dating professional knowledge and skill as well as introducing new areas of knowledge and practice. It could become a central means of reaching personnel at all levels of education and experience. Continuing education under university auspices has better access to scarce resources of skilled teaching personnel and specialists. The content as well as the patterns by which it is offered can be variously designed to reach the different manpower levels. Courses can be offered to the social work community at large or on a contract basis to large agencies to meet their staff needs. Such educational programs need to be promoted and, because experimentation with content and format is an important feature, built-in evaluative research in regard to effectiveness in reaching educational objectives should be fostered. No one segment of the educational enterprise can meet the educational needs for manpower in family planning. All levels of training and education need to be engaged with continuing clarification of the relevant levels of education for the changing and differing roles and tasks in practice.

PART IV : Program and Participants

PROGRAM AND PARTICIPANTS

PARTICIPANTS AT THE INTERNATIONAL CONFERENCE ON SOCIAL WORK EDUCATION, POPULATION, AND FAMILY PLANNING*

ARGENTINA
Miss Angela T. Vigetti, Director
Escuela de Servicio Social
San Martin 2337, Santa Fe

AUSTRALIA
Prof. Thomas Brennan, Director
Department of Social Work
University of Sydney
Sydney, N.S.W.

BRAZIL
Prof. Nadir G. Kfouri, Director
Social Work Curriculum Department
School of Social Work
Catholic University, Sao Paulo

CANADA
Serge Mongeau, M.D., Director
Le Centre de Planification Familiale
4465 Blvd. St. Laurent
Montreal, 131 (Quebec)

Dr. Benjamin Schlesinger, Professor
School of Social Work
University of Toronto
Toronto (Ontario)

CHILE
Miss Monica Gonzales, Director
Department of Social Design and Social Action
Valparaiso

COLOMBIA
Prof. Cecilia Angel, Dean
Social Work Faculty
Universidad Pontificia Bolivariana
Medellin

Antonio Ordoñez Plaja, M.D.
Minister of Public Health
Palacio de los Ministerios
Bogota D.E.

ETHIOPIA
Mr. Seyoùm G. Selassie, Dean
School of Social Work
Haile Selassie I University
Addis Ababa

GHANA
Mr. E. Q. Blavo
Lecturer in Social Administration
Department of Sociology
University of Ghana, Legon

HONG KONG
Mrs. Bella Zi Bell, Student Research Associate
Population Studies Unit
School of Public Health
University of Hawaii
Honolulu, Hawaii 96822

Miss Pearl Huang, Student
School of Social Work
University of Hawaii
Honolulu, Hawaii 96822

Miss Hei-man Lee, Head
Department of Social Work
Chung Chi College
The Chinese University of Hong Kong

INDIA
Mr. V. Gopalan, Director
Family Planning Evaluation Study
Programme Evaluation Organization
Planning Commission
464 Yojana Bhavan, New Delhi

Dr. M. S. Gore, Director
Tata Institute of Social Sciences
Deonar, Bombay 88

Mrs. Usha Modak, Director
Family Service Centre
Institute of Social Service
Nirmala Niketan
38, New Marine Lines, Bombay 1

**Affiliations listed for participants are those at the time of the conference.*

Shri Meher C. Nanavatty
Adviser Social Welfare
Ministry of Community
Development
Delhi

Prof. Shankar H. Pathak
Senior Lecturer
Delhi School of Social Work
3 University Road, Delhi 7

Mr. V. Sundarasen, Student
School of Social Work
University of Hawaii
Honolulu, Hawaii 96822

INDONESIA
Mrs. Marida Johansjah
U.N. Fellow in Social Work
University of Hawaii
Honolulu, Hawaii 96822

Mr. Christiaan L. Rudolph, Head
Social Work Department
Faculty of Social Sciences
University of Indonesia
Djakarta

Dr. Selo Soemardjan, Dean
Faculty of Social Sciences
University of Indonesia
Djakarta

IRAN
Miss Sattareh Farman-Farmaian
Director
Teheran School of Social Work
P.O.B. 2851, Teheran

ISRAEL
Mrs. Charlotte Salzberger
Senior Lecturer
Paul Baerwald School of
Social Work
Hebrew University, Jerusalem

JAMAICA
Mrs. Sybil E. Francis
Staff Tutor in Social Work
Extra Mural Department
University of the West Indies
Mona P.O., Kingston 7

JAPAN
Prof. Yuichi Nakamura, Dean
The Japan School of Social Work
1-4-9, Jingumae
Shibuya-ku, Tokyo

KOREA
Miss Myungja Chang, Student
School of Social Work
University of Hawaii
Honolulu, Hawaii 96822

Miss Kyung-Mi Cho, Student
School of Social Work
University of Hawaii
Honolulu, Hawaii 96822

Mr. Sang-Nak Ha, Chief
Social Work Department
College of Liberal Arts & Sciences
Seoul National University, Seoul

PAKISTAN
Dr. Aquila Kiani, Head
Departments of Social Work
and Sociology
University of Karachi
Karachi, West Pakistan

Dr. Rifat Rashid, Director
Department of Social Work
University of the Panjab
Lahore, West Pakistan

PERU
Miss Gloria Abate
Associated Professor
San Marcos University
Madrid-468-C, Miraflores, Lima

PHILIPPINES
Dr. Angelina C. Almanzor, Director
The Philippine School of
Social Work
Philippine Women's University
Manila

Miss Ofelia Buluran, Student
School of Social Work
University of Hawaii
Honolulu, Hawaii 96822

Rosa R. Echevarria, M.D., Student
School of Public Health
University of Hawaii
Honolulu, Hawaii 96822

Mrs. Luz A. von Einsiedel
Director
Institute of Social Work
and Community Development
University of the Philippines
Diliman, Quezon City

Dr. Soledad Florendo, Director
College of Social Work
Centro Escolar University
Manila

Miss Petra R. de Joya
Undersecretary for Program
Department of Social Welfare
San Rafael, Manila

Lourdes Leuterio, M.D., Student
School of Public Health
University of Hawaii
Honolulu, Hawaii 96822

Miss Teresita L. Silva, Director
Bureau of Family Welfare
Department of Social Welfare
San Rafael, Manila

SINGAPORE
Maggie Lim, M.D.
Education and Information Officer
International Planned Parenthood
Federation
Regional Office
26 Dunearn Road, Singapore 11

THAILAND
Miss Nuannard Amatayakul, Head
Social Work Department
Faculty of Social Administration
Thammasat University, Bangkok

Miss S. Sudara, Student
School of Social Work
University of Hawaii
Honolulu, Hawaii 96822

Miss Somsong Yontraraksa
Social Worker Supervisor
Bureau of Public Health
Bangkok Municipality, Bangkok

TURKEY
Miss Sema Kut, Director
Social Service Academy
Halk Sokak 7, Sihhiye, Ankara

UGANDA
Mr. Eric P. Kibuka, Principal
Nsamizi Training Centre
P.O. Box 92, Entebbe

UNITED ARAB REPUBLIC
Mrs. Laila S. Shukruz El Hamamsy
Director and Senior Research
Associate
Social Research Center
American University in Cairo, Cairo

UNITED KINGDOM
Miss Joan L. M. Eyden
Senior Lecturer in Social
Administration
University of Nottingham
Nottingham, NG7 2RD, England

UNITED STATES
Dr. Herbert H. Aptekar, Dean
School of Social Work
University of Hawaii
Honolulu, Hawaii 96822

Joseph D. Beasley, M.D.
President and Director
Family Planning, Inc.
136 South Derbigny Street
New Orleans, La. 70112

Dr. Winifred Bell, Professor
School of Social Welfare
State University of New York
at Albany
Albany, N. Y. 12203

Dr. Werner W. Boehm, Dean
Graduate School of Social Work
Rutgers, The State University
New Brunswick, N. J. 08903

Rev. B. J. Coughlin, Dean
School of Social Service
St. Louis University
St. Louis, Mo. 63108

Edwin F. Daily, M.D., Director
Maternity-Infant Care
Family Planning Projects
City of New York, Department
of Health
40 Worth Street
New York, N. Y. 10013

Mrs. Bess Dana
Associate Professor
Department of Community Medicine
Mt. Sinai School of Medicine
19 East 98th Street
New York, N. Y. 10029

Dr. Paul Demeny, Director
East-West Population Institute
East-West Center
University of Hawaii
Honolulu, Hawaii 96822

Mr. James R. Dumpson, Dean
School of Social Service
Fordham University at
Lincoln Center
New York, N. Y. 10023

Miss Elizabeth M. Edmands
Associate Professor
Maternal and Child Health
School of Public Health
University of North Carolina
Chapel Hill, N. C. 27514

Miss Charlotte Ellis
Program Officer
Research Division, Office
of Population
Agency for International
Development
Department of State
Washington, D.C. 20523

Dr. Harvey L. Gochros, Professor
Division of Social Work
West Virginia University
Morgantown, W. Va. 26506

Mrs. Joanna Gorman, Lecturer
School of Public Health
University of California, Berkeley
Berkeley, Cal. 94720

Miss Geraldine Gourley
Associate Professor
Maternal and Child Health
School of Public Health
University of North Carolina
Chapel Hill, N. C. 27514

Alan F. Guttmacher, M.D.
President, Planned Parenthood
Federation of America
515 Madison Avenue
New York, N. Y. 10022

Mrs. Madrid T. Hamilton
Western Regional Representative
Family Service Association
of America
821 Market Street
San Francisco, Cal. 94103

Miss Florence Haselkorn, Professor
School of Social Work
Adelphi University
Garden City, N. Y. 11530

Andrew Haynal, M.D.
School of Public Health
Loma Linda University
Riverside, Cal. 92505

Mr. Gerald M. Holden, Lecturer
School of Social Work
University of North Carolina
Chapel Hill, N. C. 27514

Mrs. Nina Horry, Director
Family Life Project
National Urban League
55 East 52nd Street
New York, N. Y. 10022

E. Ross Jenney, M.D.
Medical Consultant
East-West Population Institute
University of Hawaii
Honolulu, Hawaii 96822

Miss Mary Catherine Jennings
Chief
International Training Programs
Social and Rehabilitation Service
Department of Health, Education
and Welfare
Washington, D. C. 20201

Dr. Katherine A. Kendall
Director
Division of International Education
Council on Social Work Education
345 East 46th Street
New York, N. Y. 10017

Dr. Y. Kim, Director
Population Research Laboratory
College of Social Sciences
Utah State University
Logan, Utah 84321

Mrs. Anne M. Kinney
Distinguished Lecturer
Graduate Schools of Social Work
and Public Health
University of Pittsburgh
Pittsburgh, Pa. 15213

Mrs. Kazu Kumabe
Associate Professor
School of Social Work
University of Hawaii
Honolulu, Hawaii 96822

Dr. Richard G. Lawrence, Dean
Graduate School of Social Service
Indiana University — Purdue
University at Indianapolis
Indianapolis, Ind. 46204

Dr. Alton A. Linford, Professor
The School of Social Service
Administration
University of Chicago
Chicago, Ill. 60637

Mrs. Miriam T. Manisoff, Director
Professional Education
Planned Parenthood-World
Population
515 Madison Avenue
New York, N. Y. 10022

Dr. Rosa C. Marin, Director
Beatriz Lasalle Graduate School
of Social Work
University of Puerto Rico
Rio Piedras, P. R. 00931

Dr. Y. Scott Matsumoto
Associate Professor
School of Public Health
University of Hawaii
Honolulu, Hawaii 96822

Dr. K. Mukundarao
Associate Professor
Kent School of Social Work
University of Louisville
Louisville, Ky. 40203

Mrs. Katherine B. Oettinger
Consultant
Council on Social Work Education
345 East 46th Street
New York, N. Y. 10017

Clifford A. Pease, M.D.
Associate Director
Technical Assistance Division
The Population Council
245 Park Avenue
New York, N. Y. 10017

Dr. Ruby B. Pernell, Professor
School of Applied Social Sciences
Case Western Reserve University
Cleveland, Ohio 44106

Mrs. Harriet F. Pilpel
Chief Counsel
Planned Parenthood-World
Population
Greenbaum, Wolff and Ernst
437 Madison Avenue
New York, N. Y. 10022

Dr. Arnulf M. Pins
Executive Director
Council on Social Work Education
345 East 46th Street
New York, N. Y. 10017

Dr. Bernice Polemis, Professor
School of Social Work
University of Hawaii
Honolulu, Hawaii 96822

Dr. Ward Porter, Acting Chief
Division of Intramural Research
Office of Research, Demonstrations
and Training
Social and Rehabilitation Service
Department of Health, Education
and Welfare
Washington, D. C. 20201

Miss Lydia Rapoport, Professor
School of Social Welfare
University of California, Berkeley
Berkeley, Cal. 94720

Reimert T. Ravenholt, M.D.
Director
Office of Population
Technical Assistance Bureau
Agency for International
Development
Department of State
Washington, D. C. 20523

Ralph Sachs, M.D., Professor
School of Public Health
University of Hawaii
Honolulu, Hawaii 96822

Dr. Irwin T. Sanders, Chairman
Department of Sociology
Boston University
Boston, Mass.

Dr. Mildred Sikkema, Professor
School of Social Work
University of Hawaii
Honolulu, Hawaii 96822

Dr. Herman D. Stein, Provost
Case Western Reserve University
Cleveland, Ohio 44106

Dr. Betty Stirling
Associate Professor
Department of Sociology
and Anthropology
Loma Linda University
Riverside, Cal. 92505

Miss Alix Szilasi
Administrative Assistant
Council on Social Work Education
345 East 46th Street
New York, N. Y. 10017

Mrs. Alice M. Varela, Director
Social Service Division
Health Insurance Plan of
Greater New York
625 Madison Avenue
New York, N. Y. 10022

E. Voulgaropoulos, M.D., Head
International Health/
Population Unit
School of Public Health
University of Hawaii
Honolulu, Hawaii 96822

Dr. Ellen Winston
Social Welfare Policy Consultant
1712 Piccadilly Lane
Raleigh, N. C. 27608

Dr. Robert Wolff
Associate Professor
School of Public Health
University of Hawaii
Honolulu, Hawaii 96822

YUGOSLAVIA
Dr. Eugen Pusic, Professor
Public Administration
School of Law
University of Zagreb, Zagreb

ORGANIZATION OF
AMERICAN STATES
Mrs. Eliana de Cataldo, Specialist
Program of Community
Development and Social Welfare
Department of Social Affairs
Pan American Union
Washington, D. C. 20006

UNITED NATIONS
Miss Aida Gindy, Chief
Social Welfare Services Section
Social Development Division
United Nations
New York, N. Y. 10017

Dr. Milos Macura, Director
Population Division
United Nations
New York, N. Y. 10017

ADVISORY COMMITTEE*

Chairman: Dr. Ruby B. Pernell

Rev. B. J. Coughlin, S.J., Dean
School of Social Service
St. Louis University, Missouri

Edwin F. Daily, M.D., Director
Family Planning Projects
Maternity and Infant Care
New York City Department of Health
(representing American Public Health Association)

Miss Elizabeth M. Edmands, R.N.
Associate Professor
Carolina Population Center
University of North Carolina

Alan F. Guttmacher, M.D., President
Planned Parenthood-World Population
New York, New York

Dr. Dorothy Lally, Assistant Chief for International Cooperation
Department of Health, Education, and Welfare, Washington, D. C.

Dr. K. Mukundarao, Associate Professor
Kent School of Social Work
University of Louisville, Kentucky

Clifford A. Pease, M.D., Deputy Assistant
The Population Council, New York

Dr. Ruby B. Pernell, Professor
School of Applied Social Sciences
Case Western Reserve University
Cleveland,Ohio

Mrs. Harriet F. Pilpel, Chief Counsel
Planned Parenthood-World Population
New York, New York

Miss Lydia Rapoport, Professor
School of Social Welfare
University of California, Berkeley

Dr. Harold A. Richman, Dean
School of Social Service Administration
University of Chicago, Illinois

Dr. Irwin T. Sanders, Chairman
Department of Sociology
Boston University, Massachusetts

Dr. Joseph Speidel, Acting Chief
Research Division, Office of Population
Agency for International Development
Washington, D. C.

Charles S. Sprague, M.D., Dean
Southwestern Medical School
University of Texas, Dallas
(representing Association of American Medical Colleges)

Dr. Herman D. Stein, Provost
Case Western Reserve University
Cleveland, Ohio
(representing International Association of Schools of Social Work)

Dr. Ellen Winston, Social Policy Consultant
Raleigh, North Carolina

United Nations Advisers

Miss Aida Gindy, Chief
Social Welfare Services Section
Social Development Division
United Nations
(Also representing UNICEF)

Mr. P. S. Menon, Officer in charge of Population Programs and Projects, Population Division
United Nations

**Affiliations listed are those at the time of the conference.*

CONSULTANTS AND CONTRIBUTORS

American Friends Service Committee
Family Planning Program
Philadelphia, Pennsylvania

American Public Health Association
Family Planning Program
New York, New York

Association of American Medical Colleges
Washington, D. C.

Carolina Population Center
University of North Carolina
Chapel Hill, North Carolina

Columbia University
International Institute for Study of Human Reproduction
New York, New York

Family Service Association of America, Inc.
New York, New York

Ford Foundation
Population Program
New York, New York

National Institute for Child Health and Human Development
Washington, D. C.

Planned Parenthood-World Population
New York, New York

Population Council
New York, New York

Population Crisis Committee
Washington, D. C.

Population Reference Bureau
Washington, D. C.

Sex Information and Education Council of the United States
New York, New York

U.S. Department of Health, Education, and Welfare
Social and Rehabilitation Service
Washington, D. C.

East-West Center Liaison

Dr. Paul Demeny, Director
East-West Population Institute

Mr. Jack Durham, Conference Officer
East-West Center

E. Ross Jenney, M.D., Medical Consultant
East-West Population Institute

Dr. Mildred Sikkema, Professor
School of Social Work, University of Hawaii

CSWE Staff

Dr. Katherine A. Kendall
Project Director

Mrs. Louise N. Mumm
Conference Assistant

Mrs. Katherine B. Oettinger
Conference Consultant

Miss Alix Szilasi
Administrative Assistant

Conference Rapporteur and Analyst

Dr. Herman D. Stein
Rapporteur

Dr. Irwin T. Sanders
Analyst

PROGRAM

Monday, March 9, 1970 **East-West Center**

1:00 P.M.-2:00 P.M. — Registration

2:00 P.M.-3:00 P.M. — Opening Ceremonies

Presiding: Dr. Everett Kleinjans, Chancellor
East-West Center

Greetings: Dr. Paul Demeny, Director
East-West Population Institute, East-West Center

Dr. Alton A. Linford, President
Council on Social Work Education (CSWE)

Dr. Herman D. Stein, President
International Association of Schools of Social Work (IASSW)

3:30 P.M.-4:00 P.M. — Organization Session

Presiding: Dr. Katherine A. Kendall, Project Director
Council on Social Work Education

Conference Plans: Mrs. Katherine B. Oettinger, Conference Consultant
Council on Social Work Education

4:00 P.M.-5:00 P.M. — Organization Meetings of Discussion Groups

5:30 P.M.-7:00 P.M. — Informal Buffet Supper
East-West Center, University of Hawaii

7:30 P.M. — OPENING SESSION — PUBLIC MEETING

Greetings: His Excellency John A. Burns, Governor of Hawaii

Presiding: Dr. Harlan Cleveland, President
University of Hawaii

Subject: POPULATION AND FAMILY PLANNING: A WORLD-WIDE VIEW OF A UNIVERSAL PROBLEM

Speaker: Dr. Milos Macura, Director
Population Division, United Nations

Subject: SOCIAL WORK ROLES AND OPPORTUNITIES FOR SERVICE

Speaker: Miss Aida Gindy, Chief
Social Welfare Services Section, United Nations

Tuesday, March 10, 1970 **East-West Center**

9:00 A.M.-12:00 Noon — PLENARY SESSION

THEME FOR THE DAY: PERSPECTIVES ON POPULATION DYNAMICS, FAMILY PLANNING AND ATTITUDINAL CHANGE

The papers prepared by the three speakers will be available at the time of registration for advance study by the delegates. In the plenary session, each speaker will present a 15-minute summary of the highlights of his paper and pose major issues for discussion from the floor and subsequent consideration in the discussion groups.

Presiding: Dr. Herman D. Stein, Conference Rapporteur

Subject: PERSPECTIVES ON NATIONAL APPROACHES — GOVERNMENTAL LEADERSHIP

Speaker: Antonio Ordoñez Plaja, M.D.
Colombia Minister of Public Health

Subject: PERSPECTIVES ON NATIONAL APPROACHES — VOLUNTARY LEADERSHIP

Speaker: Alan F. Guttmacher, M.D., President
Planned Parenthood-World Population

Subject: PERSPECTIVES ON ATTITUDINAL CHANGE

Speaker: Dr. Selo Soemardjan, Professor of Sociology
University of Indonesia

Questions and Discussion

1:30 P.M.-2:30 P.M. — Summary

Subject: PERSPECTIVES: THE PROGRAMMATIC CONTEXT FOR EDUCATION AND TRAINING IN SOCIAL WORK

Speaker: Dr. Herman D. Stein

2:30 P.M.-4:40 P.M. — Meeting of Discussion Groups

All groups, which will be interdisciplinary in composition, will produce educational recommendations for social work related to the central conference theme:

EDUCATION OF SOCIAL WORKERS TO CONTRIBUTE TO ATTITUDINAL CHANGE AND MORE EFFECTIVE SERVICE IN POPULATION AND FAMILY PLANNING

The theme will be explored in the light of current and anticipated SOCIAL WORK ROLES AND FUNCTIONS related to population and family planning. Three groups will emphasize specific categories of functions or service and one group will deal with general issues in the development and utilization of social work manpower.

DISCUSSION GROUPS

A. — THE SOCIAL WORKER IN SOCIAL POLICY AND SOCIAL PLANNING

Chairman: Dr. James R. Dumpson, Dean
School of Social Service
Fordham University, New York

Recorder: Dr. Winifred Bell, Professor
School of Social Welfare
State University of New York, Albany

B. — THE SOCIAL WORKER IN PROGRAM DEVELOPMENT AND EXECUTION

Chairman: Dr. Arnulf M. Pins, Executive Director
Council on Social Work Education, New York

Recorder: Mrs. Joanna Gorman, Lecturer
School of Public Health
University of California, Berkeley

C. — SOCIAL WORK SERVICE TO INDIVIDUALS, FAMILIES, GROUPS, AND COMMUNITIES

Chairman: Dr. Herbert H. Aptekar, Dean
School of Social Work
University of Hawaii

Co-Chairman: Miss Florence Haselkorn, Professor
School of Social Work
Adelphi University, New York

Recorder: Miss Geraldine Gourley
School of Public Health
University of North Carolina

D. — DEPLOYMENT AND UTILIZATION OF SOCIAL WORK MANPOWER

Chairman: Dr. Ellen Winston, Social Policy Consultant
Raleigh, North Carolina

Recorder: Dr. Richard G. Lawrence, Dean
Graduate School of Social Service
Indiana University, Indianapolis

Wednesday, March 11, 1970 **East-West Center**

8:30 A.M.-12:00 Noon — PLENARY SESSION

8:30 A.M.-10:30 — Panel Discussion

Introductions: Dr. Ruby B. Pernell, Chairman
Conference Advisory Committee

Subject: INTER-PROFESSIONAL DIALOGUE ON THE SOCIAL DIMENSIONS OF THE PROBLEM: THE SOCIAL WORK TASK

Moderator: Mrs. Bess Dana, Associate Professor
Department of Community Medicine
Mt. Sinai School of Medicine, New York
— Social Work

Panel Participants: Joseph D. Beasley, M.D., President and Director
Family Planning, Inc., New Orleans, Louisiana
— Medicine and Public Health

Dr. Laila S. El Hamamsy, Director and Senior Research Associate, Social Research Center
American University in Cairo, U.A.R.
— Anthropology

Mr. E. P. Kibuka, Principal
Nsamizi Training Centre
Entebbe, Uganda
— Community Development

Mrs. Harriet F. Pilpel, Chief Counsel
Planned Parenthood-World Population, New York
— Law

Dr. Eugen Pusic, Professor
University of Zagreb, Yugoslavia
— Public Administration

11:00 A.M.-12:00 Noon — INTERPROFESSIONAL COLLABORATION IN CLINICAL PRACTICE — A film presentation

Commentator: Miss Lydia Rapoport, Professor
School of Social Welfare, University of California, Berkeley

1:30 P.M.-3:30 P.M. — Meeting of Discussion Groups

6:00 P.M.-8:00 P.M. — RECEPTION — "College Hill", Residence of President Cleveland

Thursday, March 12, 1970 **East-West Center**

9:00 A.M.-3:00 P.M. — Final Meetings of Discussion Groups

9:00 A.M-10:30 A.M. — PLENARY SESSION

Presiding: Dr. Ruby B. Pernell

Subject: THE GROUPS REPORT

Participants: Group A: Dean James R. Dumpson
Group B: Dr. Arnulf M. Pins
Group C: Miss Florence Haselkorn
Group D: Dr. Ellen Winston

Floor Discussion

11:00 A.M.-12:00 Noon

Presiding: Reimert T. Ravenholt, M.D., Director
Office of Population, Agency for International Development

Subject: THE RAPPORTEUR REPORTS

Speaker: Dr. Herman D. Stein

12:00 Noon-12:30 P.M. — Closing Ceremony

Recognition of Contributions, Talents, and Services
Dr. Katherine A. Kendall

Aloha! E. Ross Jenney, M.D.
East-West Population Institute